Before I Forget

Before I Forget

An Illustrated Autobiography
of Murray J. Harris

MURRAY J. HARRIS

RESOURCE *Publications* · Eugene, Oregon

BEFORE I FORGET
An Illustrated Autobiography of Murray J. Harris

Copyright © 2019 Murray J. Harris. All rights reserved. Except for brief quotations in critical publications or reviews, no part of this book may be reproduced in any manner without prior written permission from the publisher. Write: Permissions, Wipf and Stock Publishers, 199 W. 8th Ave., Suite 3, Eugene, OR 97401.

Resource Publications
An Imprint of Wipf and Stock Publishers
199 W. 8th Ave., Suite 3
Eugene, OR 97401

www.wipfandstock.com

PAPERBACK ISBN: 978-1-5326-7052-7
HARDCOVER ISBN: 978-1-5326-7053-4
EBOOK ISBN: 978-1-5326-7054-1

JUNE 3, 2021

To
my many friends
throughout the world
who have inspired me in countless ways

Contents

Photos and Illustrations | xi

Preface | xiii

1   **Family, Marriage, and Special Friends** | 1
   Family | 1
   Marriage | 4
   Special Friends | 4

2   **Education** | 8
   Remuera Primary (= Elementary) School | 8
   Auckland Grammar School | 8
   Auckland Teachers' College | 12
   University of Auckland | 13
   University of London | 14
   University of Otago | 15
   University of Manchester | 15
   Life in Manchester | 18

3   **Teaching Career (I)** | 22
   Auckland Teachers' College (1956–57) | 22
   Meadowbank Primary School (1958) | 22
   Glendowie Primary School (1959–60) | 23
   Glendowie College (1962–65, 1970) | 24

4   **Teaching Career (II)** | 26
   1967–68 at Trinity Evangelical Divinity School (TEDS) | 27
   1971–78 at TEDS | 28

Contents

5   **Teaching Career (III) | 34**
1986–97 at TEDS | 34

6   **Teaching Career (IV) | 41**
The Bible College of New Zealand (BCNZ) (1978–81) | 41

7   **Teaching Career (V): Tyndale House (TH) and the University of Cambridge (1981–86) | 46**
History and influence of Tyndale House (TH) | 46
Appointment to the Wardenship of TH | 48
Teaching and relationship with the University | 49
Responsibilities of the Warden | 50
Highlights from our TH years | 51
Family during our TH years | 53

8   **Teaching Career (VI) | 55**
Visiting Lectureships | 55

9   **Adjusting to life in the USA: "Kiwis in the Land of the Eagle" | 59**
Immigration Issues | 59
Language differences | 60
American Customs | 61
American Humor | 62

10   **Writing Ventures | 64**
General observations | 64
Apologetic writing | 65
Evangelistic writing | 69

11   **Happy Memories | 72**
Family | 72
Colleagues | 72
Students | 73
New International Version (NIV) involvement | 74
Creation of Tyndale College (TC) in New Zealand | 77

Contents

Library gift to the Nairobi Evangelical Graduate School of Theology (NEGST) | 81
Publisher's preface in the Exegetical Guide to the Greek New Testament (EGGNT) | 82
Support of needy children | 84
Billy Graham campaign | 84
Move to a retirement village | 85

12 Painful Memories | 86
Death of our daughter Susan | 87
Jennifer's diagnosis of multiple sclerosis (MS) | 88
The Dr Norman L. Geisler controversy | 88

13 Disappointments | 91
International Fellowship of Evangelical Theologians (IFET) | 92
The New Testament from 28 Translations | 93
Inability to establish a regular holiday venue near home | 93
Finding God at the University of Auckland (?) | 94

14 Reflections on God and his guidance | 95
God is a God of serendipities, who delights to give us unexpected, pleasant surprises. | 95
God is the Sovereign Lord, who graciously orchestrates the details of our lives, shutting some doors and opening others. | 96
The mystery of God's will | 96

Appendix | 99
Chronology | 99
Membership of Learned Societies | 100
Selected Writing | 101

Photos and Illustrations

Frontispiece: Murray and Jennifer

1. Leslie and Jessie Harris, their five sons and their wives | 2
2. Jack and Jessie McCracken, Jennifer at nursing graduation | 5
3. Dr Kenneth and Ruth Kantzer, David Burt, Dr Graham Smith | 7
4. Prose composition for MA honors degree in Latin | 14
5. University Library cards for Manchester and Oxford | 17
6. Man of the Year 1973 | 29
7. Camel ride in Jerusalem, family in 1981 | 30
8. US copyright for game of "Smudge" | 36
9. University of Otago Open Lecture, 1993 | 37
10. Suggested mottos for Trinity International University | 39
11. Murray J. Harris Scholarship award, 1997 | 39
12. Murray and Jennifer on Empire State, nappy sketch for Murray | 42
13. Oliver and Jane as youngsters | 44
14. Tyndale House Library Extension opening, 1985 | 47
15. Life of Brian pamphlet | 70
16. Committee on Bible Translation (NIV), British subcommittee | 77
17. My worksheet for revision of Romans | 79
18. Introducing Tyndale College | 80
19. Murray and Jennifer with Dr David Kasali, inserts for NEGST library gifts | 82
20. Quilted banners for NEGST, Billy Graham Crusade counsellor badge, 1959 | 84
21. Sample quilts for premature babies | 88

Preface

ANYONE RASH ENOUGH TO consider writing their autobiography needs to face two pertinent issues. First: "Does not a person writing their own biography suffer from megalomania, an inflated view of their importance or significance? Should they not let someone else decide after their departure whether a biography is likely to be profitable to readers?"

It all depends on the motive for writing. In my case, I am keen to show how God can graciously shape a quiet, unsuspecting young Kiwi from Down Under to become useful in his worldwide plans. Never did I imagine, in my wildest dreams in those early years, that I would be privileged to travel around the world, teach at the graduate level in New Zealand, Britain, Germany and the USA, and work alongside world renowned scholars. After all, I simply began my teaching career at the ripe old age of eighteen with thirty-two eight-year olds in an insignificant city in the remote South Pacific! Whether my autobiography is tainted by megalomania is for the reader to determine, but I hope not. Inevitably, however, the personal pronoun "I" will occur all too frequently.

Second: "Why not wait until you are well into your 80's or beyond, when the possibility of further travel and service outside New Zealand is greatly reduced? After all, your eldest brother is now ninety-eight!"

In reply, let me observe that I am perilously close to becoming an octogenarian, and that I am now a happy fulltime caregiver for my wife of fifty–five years who has suffered from multiple sclerosis for over thirty years, so that travel for us is out of the question. We attend church together on Sundays but Jennifer is able to manage little more than that. Also, I now have access to specialised information and unique memories that may well disappear or fade with the passing of the years.

Not infrequently, those with an inclination to write have kept meticulous diaries, with copious detail about people, places and dates. My diaries

Preface

have always contained only upcoming events and responsibilities, not careful records of things past. Perhaps in compensation I have kept hundreds of memorabilia items—from my Primary (Elementary) School certificate and Secondary (High) School class lists and term reports, through to the Murray J. Harris Scholarship announcement and advertisements of special University lectures I have given. In keeping with this, my autobiography is well illustrated with memorabilia, many humorous, some unique, but hopefully all interesting.

One further apology for my approach. Most autobiographies are arranged chronologically, beginning with family roots and finishing with late in life episodes. But I have chosen to arrange my material topically, so that readers can immediately go to sections that may have special interest or relevance to them—such as "Adjusting to Life in the USA" or "Reflections on God's Guidance." For those who prefer a chronological approach, there is an Appendix listing dates and events, and selected writing, all in chronological sequence.

Some may think that an autobiography should be called "As I Remember" or "In Retrospect," but perversely I have opted for "Before I Forget"—a hint at advancing years and the memory loss that often follows.

Let me state at the outset my aim in writing this relatively brief autobiography. It seeks to bring encouragement to several groups of fellow Christians.

1. To encourage young people to excel in their studies, whatever their area of specialization.
2. To encourage married believers to be faithful to their spouses, whatever the future holds with regard to their health.
3. To encourage believers to be creative in their defence and spread of the Good News, and to maintain a worldview in their giving.
4. To encourage graduates of tertiary institutions to become knowledgeable in the Faith and to be involved in their local churches.
5. To encourage all believers to recognize God's guiding hand in their lives as the God of serendipities and as the Sovereign Lord.

I would like to express my warm gratitude to Matthew Wimer, George Callihan, and the whole team at Wipf and Stock for their efficient service in producing this book.

I

Family, Marriage, and Special Friends

FAMILY

WHEN PEOPLE ASK ME for my date of birth and I respond March 19, 1939, I immediately assure them that my birth had nothing to do with the outbreak of World War II later that year. Rumour has it that I was supposed to be Janice, since my mother had seven younger brothers and then four sons of her own (Bruce, Evan, Don, and Robin)!

Except for one lonely brother (Robin) who was an accountant, all our family were teachers. Both of my parents—Arthur Leslie and Jessie Melville (née Fairgray)—attended Teachers' College in Auckland and my father taught in various schools throughout the North Island of New Zealand, often serving as Headmaster (= Principal). My eldest brother, Bruce, studied classics first at Auckland University and then as a Rhodes Scholar at Balliol College of Oxford University, before returning to New Zealand to teach at Auckland University and subsequently at Macquarie University in Sydney where he ended his teaching career as Head of the School of History, Philosophy and Politics. Evan served with distinction in various primary and secondary schools in the north of the North Island, including a period at a missionary school in Popondetta in New Guinea. Both of these older brothers served abroad with the Armed Forces for five years in World War II, just as my father had served in World War I until returning home wounded from Passchendaele. My third older brother, Don, began his legal studies at the University of Auckland before becoming the Vinerian Scholar in law at Oxford University, cofounder and formerly Director of the Centre for Socio-Legal Studies at Oxford, and Emeritus Fellow of Balliol College there.

So it came as no great surprise to anyone when I chose to prepare for the noble profession at Teachers' College at Epsom in Auckland at the age of 16 years 10 months, not having sufficient money for fulltime study at the University. So began a 14-year stint at various universities (Auckland, London, Otago, Manchester), with nine of these years being part-time and study at two of these institutions (Otago and London) being extra-mural.

Leslie and Jessie Harris

Given the 18-year difference between my age and that of my brother Bruce, and his absence abroad for study and war service, it was only as an adolescent living with him and his family while my parents were on a world trip after Dad's retirement that I began to become acquainted with him. With only six years between myself and Robin in age, it was natural that I was closest to him. He excelled as a rugby player—"first five" was his specialist position—representing University, New Zealand Universities, Auckland and the North Island in that position. It is possible that he was overlooked for an All Black tour because it was known that he would not play on Sundays.

Left to right, Robin, Evan, Murray, Bruce, Don, Patricia, Leone, Jennifer, Pam, Jacqueline

Two particular episodes involving Robin stand out in my memory. On one occasion Dad and I travelled down to Hamilton for a "Ranfurly Shield" rugby game between Auckland and Waikato to watch Robin in action in a crucially important game. Auckland won the rather dour match, by 9 to 6 as I remember, and gained the Shield amid much jubilation (only to lose it the following Saturday!). But what fascinated me even more was to read in the evening news that night (the "Eight O'Clock") that the rugby commentator regarded Harris as having "beautiful hands," because he was able to catch any ball, high or low, that the halfback threw at him.

The second episode reflects the fact that of the five boys in our family, the first and fourth—Bruce and Robin—were the epitome of politeness and good behavior, while the other three of us were the rascals. When asked, my mother would openly say, "Murray is a *naughty* boy." Accordingly, when it became apparent that Murray would sometimes use "bloody" as a swear word, Dad (rather unwisely) told Robin that he must report to him any time he heard Murray use that frightful word! Clearly the use of the strap would result. Poor Robin, when Murray once let his guard drop! What was he to do? Obey his father and report the lapse, or protect his younger brother from the wrath to come? I remember holding Robin by the feet, pleading with him not to report me to headquarters! What was the outcome? As I remember, Robin felt he was honour-bound to tell Dad, but added "Murray is *very, very* sorry and promises he will *never ever* use that word again"!

Our family heritage was outstanding. We were encouraged in our schoolwork and our sporting pursuits. Our parents taught us Christian truth and Christian morals, and themselves embodied a Christian lifestyle and world view for us to follow. For fifty years my father served on the NZ Council of the SIM (Sudan Interior Mission, as it was then called), for many of those years as chairman. Theirs was an informed conservatism with openness to new ideas and approaches. For example, along with a distinguished businessman, Leo Clarke, my father began Every Boy's Rally, a Scout-like boys' movement that was linked to the local church, and that soon spread to several other countries and became the pattern for Every Girl's Rally. When I was twelve I made a formal profession of faith in Christ at a boys' camp but I was probably a believer before then. I have often said that proof of life comes not through producing one's birth certificate from the attic but through showing the vital signs of appetite in the kitchen—desire for God and his Word and his people.

My rich church heritage was with the Christian Brethren assemblies (sometimes known as the Open Brethren) where I found opportunities to serve as a Sunday School teacher and superintendent and as a Every Boy's Rally leader. During my university years my greatest spiritual *and* intellectual stimulation took place during the weekly Lord's Supper/Breaking of Bread service where men were encouraged to lead in worship as directed by the Spirit. This process presented an unpredictable challenge to correlate the Scriptural passages read, the hymns chosen to be sung, and the spontaneous prayers offered, particularly if one was seeking to prompt worship by participating in one of these three ways. Appropriate participation required a good knowledge of Scripture and Christian hymnody, as well as an ability to lead in public prayer.

MARRIAGE

On August 28, 1963, I married Jennifer Mary McCracken, daughter of Jack and Jessie McCracken, at Tamaki Bible Chapel in Auckland. Jennifer's father officiated at the ceremony since he was a regular marriage celebrant, while Jennifer's brother, John, "walked her down the aisle." The McCracken family were and are especially gifted artistically on the female side, and practically on the male side.

SPECIAL FRIENDS

In any biography or autobiography it is expected that the subject will identify people who have had a special influence on one's life. It is obvious that Bruce and Don blazed a shining trail in academic pursuits for their youngest brother to follow; it was to them that I dedicated what is perhaps my most specialized work, *Prepositions and Theology in the Greek New Testament*. But apart from the positive influence of my whole immediate family, mention should be made of three people.

Although *Graham Smith* and I were in the same Sunday School classes and attended the same secondary school (Auckland Grammar), it was not until we were both students at Auckland Teachers' College that our friendship blossomed. Not only were we both keen members of the Evangelical Union there, but we regularly spent our lunch hours together, pacing the footpaths of Epsom, grappling with theological issues, and, more productively, drawing up a list of the essential or desirable features of any potential female friend or marriage partner. Alongside our College studies (not too demanding!), we began studying together for the extra-mural Diploma in Theology from the University of London. When Graham took up a teaching post in Rhodesia in 1962 and we left for study in Britain in 1965, we lost touch with each other until our mutual retirement from teaching saw us both back on home territory in New Zealand in the 1990s.

Jack and Jessie McCracken

Jennifer at her nursing graduation in 1963

NZ Registered Nurse Medal

UK Registered Nurse Medal

Graham has always had an infectious zest for life, an enthusiasm for anything new, and an enviable penchant for detail, especially mathematical detail (mathematician that he is), that corresponds to my own preoccupation with grammatical detail in Greek. He taught me the art of hitchhiking on country roads and how to cope with prolonged intervals between rides! Shortly after our return to New Zealand in 1997 he graciously arranged for some Christian Trusts to purchase for us a van (a Toyota Noah (!) from

Japan) that has a ramp at the rear to accommodate Jennifer's wheelchair that can then come up adjacent to the driver's seat. We greatly appreciated this unexpected gift and continue to enjoy the use of the vehicle. In his earlier years Graham was not enamored with academic study, but in his retirement he embodied the "late developer," completing both a University of Auckland Master of Education with first class honours and in 2013 his Doctor of Education degree. It was to Graham that I dedicated the second edition of my commentary on the Greek text of Colossians and Philemon.

The three-year difference in our ages meant that *David Burt* and I were never in the same class at Ngaire Avenue Sunday School or Auckland Grammar. But University days quickly melted that difference as we both pursued our professional training—David excelling academically with a double degree in arts and law (BA and LLB) followed by a first class LLM. Year after year we both attended (with a small group of fellow debaters) regular Friday night sessions in his law office at the bottom of Queen Street, solving all of the outstanding theological problems of the ages under the stimulation of A. H. Strong's dense *Systematic Theology*. I benefitted in particular from David's penetrating legal acumen and ruthless questioning. Wide-ranging discussion also took place during the week following Easter each year—a traditional holiday for lawyers—when we scaled the four mountains of the North Island. But regular exercise occurred week after week as we played soccer and tennis in inter—church competition. Not to be forgotten was a weekend spent camping at Snells Beach, each of us with our one and only son, Murray and Oliver.

David's whole life has been marked by an exquisite predictability. He always welcomes you warmly, lends an attentive ear, gives sound advice, offers spiritual insight, and affords generous encouragement. It was a special delight during one sabbatical leave when I was giving lectures at Pathways College to surprise him with a presentation to him in the presence of his whole family of my book *Jesus as God: The New Testament Use of Theos in Reference to Jesus,* that still bears the dedication in its reprints, "To David Burt, Christian brother, Esteemed friend."

During my teaching career in the field of Biblical studies, no person has exercised a more profound influence on me than *Dr Kenneth S. Kantzer*, formerly Dean of Trinity Evangelical Divinity School in Deerfield, Illinois. Here was a distinguished Harvard doctoral graduate who throughout his administrative career surrendered his own publishing potential so that he could further the professional advancement of a myriad of younger scholars whom he chose to be teachers at Trinity. He recognised some potential in a young Kiwi teacher from "Down Under" and again and again over the years he pulled the necessary immigration strings to enable us to spend some nineteen years at this one institution on three separate occasions, even when other teaching opportunities presented themselves to us. One of Kantzer's innovations at Trinity was to create a generous sabbatical scheme of one sabbatical quarter or term after six of teaching that enabled a teacher to add the summer vacation and so create a six-month period for research and writing.

Dr. Kenneth and Ruth Kantzer

Kenneth and Ruth Kantzer unofficially adopted us as orphans half a world away from home. He accelerated my progress through the stages of advancement in American academic life—assistant professor, associate professor, full professor. This had the benefit of increases in salary! With pleasure their daughter tells us that in her advancing years her mother would affectionately refer to anyone whose name she had forgotten as "Jennifer." Also, Dr Kantzer himself said that anyone his wife took a liking to was immediately called "Jennifer." Before Dr Kantzer's illness and death I was able to give him a copy of the Acknowledgments in my one-thousand-one hundred-page tome *The Second Epistle to the Corinthians* that indicate that the volume was dedicated to him.

David Burt and Dr. Graham Smith

2

Education

REMUERA PRIMARY (= ELEMENTARY) SCHOOL

PROMINENT IN MY MEMORY of the seven years spent at this school was the weekly bus ride during the final two years when we crossed town to attend a specialized woodwork class for boys and a cooking class for girls. Also weekly in this secular school was a "Bible in Schools" class when a local pastor or young people's leader or parent came in as volunteers to share Bible stories and teaching and encourage the memorisation of key verses or passages. I won a book prize for the word-perfect recitation in front of the class of the Beatitudes in the King James Version (the only version regularly used in those days).

At the bottom of the school's large playing field was a series of irrigation trenches under bush that we enjoyed jumping over. At the beginning of the lunch hour a representative of each class would have to line up at the headmaster's window and show for his approval a leather rugby ball whose seams had just been greased with preservative fat obtained each day from a local butcher! Who knows how many All Blacks began their career with that greasy ball?

AUCKLAND GRAMMAR SCHOOL

Established in 1868, this is a state secondary (= high) school and the largest single-sex school in New Zealand. It is well known for its conservative traditions, including the compulsory study of Latin for higher stream first year students. Not surprisingly, then, the school's motto is in Latin, *Per angusta ad augusta*, "Through narrow ravines to majestic heights," or "Through difficulties to greatness." Similarly, the school song, *Insignem laudem meretur . . .* , "He deserves outstanding praise who . . ." Without a doubt the most famous old boy of "Grammar" (as it is known nationwide)—and also the most famous New Zealander—is Sir Edmund Hillary of Everest fame.

At that time most boys spent three or four years at "Grammar," from Form 3 to Form 5 or 6. A "form" is the name given to a particular year's class, and classes for each year were "streamed" according to ability, from 3A to 3G, for example. Teachers at Auckland Grammar, or "masters" as they were always called, were held in high regard, because of their fine teaching skills but also because in the early days they were permitted to use a long, flexible cane on a boy's posterior as punishment for misbehaviour.

In our first year of Latin, we would each often be asked to translate one sentence found in our textbook. Since we seated in alphabetical order in the classroom we could work out when our turn to translate a sentence would occur and could prepare "our" sentence well in advance and then peacefully relax. That is, until one morning our master, who often seemed bored and half asleep, suddenly woke up from his stupor as he read out boys' names in alphabetical order. "Daryl Forbes-Dawson—that's a double-barrelled name, isn't it? That's worth two sentences!" The panic spread quickly, especially since "Harris" was the next name! Still speaking of Latin, in year three (with the same teacher) when we were expected to translate several sentences in succession, not merely one, I remember an occasion when I thought I had proposed an eloquent rendering and looked up to the master for approval, only to have him say, "Well, go on Harris, are you waiting for applause?"

During our breaks between pairs of classes and at lunchtime, we used to play "fives" in high, three-sided concrete walls in a game like squash, but with the palm of the hand replacing a racquet. In the first week of Social Studies in Form 3, when everything was so new and daunting, we had been given some "homework" to prepare for class. Our teacher (Mr Webb) was a burly man with the build of an Olympic wrestler, known behind his back as "Spider Webb." When he discovered that a boy had failed to complete this small assignment, he bellowed out, "Come up here, boy!" and enticed him, tremblingly. to look out the window. "Do you see that dark smear over there on the fives court? That is all that remains of the last boy who did not do his homework!"

Let me fast forward to year four, the last year at Grammar. Over the years our history teacher had accumulated splendid notes on all the subjects required for examination, but he tended simply to dictate them for our recording, only pausing when a question was asked for clarification. All too often the experience illustrated the saying that a lecture could be defined as the movement of a body of information from the lecturer's notes to the student's notebook—preferably without passing through the mind of either.

One habit of our English teacher was to progress down the class list of names asking each boy to indicate the books he had recently read. Before my name came the name of Barry Gustafson, a prodigious reader who later became a notable political scientist and the Dean of an extension of the University of Auckland. When his endless list was over, and the name of Harris was called out, all I could offer was the abridged edition (!) of *The Ascent of Everest* by Sir John Hunt. "You're not keen on reading, Harris?" the teacher asked. "No, sir." Little did he know that during my last two years at high school I used to get up at 5am each morning to spend one hour in Bible reading and study and one hour in prayer.

In our Mathematics class ("Maths" in New Zealand), one pupil (we were now all sixteen or seventeen years old) was bold enough to try a painful prank on the teacher. "Streak" Nicolls was a very tall man, once an Olympic athlete, and rather uncouth in manner and language. Coming into the classroom, he would throw himself atop an empty desk facing the class and bellow out "Pudown!" which was the signal to open our books and record the next theorem. But he had become deaf as the years had passed, and was always adjusting his rather primitive hearing aids. Fordyce, the heartless prankster, held up his hand and mouthed a long question. "Streak," now in a panic and fearing that all his hearing had suddenly gone, began fruitlessly fiddling with his hearing aids!

Perhaps the master I felt closest to was George Marshall, later to become principal of a large co-ed school. In years one and four he was my French teacher. When junior students were feeling too confident of their knowledge, he would say, "Boy, what you know about French could be written on the back of a postage stamp!" During that final year, when we read *Tartarin de Tarascon* by Alphonse Daudet, I once mistakenly spoke of *casual* sentences, when I meant *causal*, so Marshall sometimes referred to me as "casual Harris"! But a clear indication of our mutual respect was my courage to write on top of an exam paper the following Latin sentence: *Tantum abest ut nostra miremur ut nobis non satisfaciant ipsi nostri magistri,*

"So far are we from admiring our own work that our teachers themselves do not satisfy us." We remained friends—and some years later when we were both pursuing a postgraduate Diploma in Education I lent him at his request my notes of some lectures he had missed.

But two of the most memorable episodes of those years involved our headmaster (= principal), Colin Littlejohn, a short, unassuming gentleman. Each morning a full assembly was held in the cavernous assembly hall that was built in the majestic Spanish Mission architectural style and holds well over one thousand people. The head prefect would march up the stairs on to the stage and wait astride until the door to the headmaster's office would open off to his right. Then, at attention, he would cry out in a voice capable of rousing the dead or the sleeping, "School!" at which everyone would stand and the headmaster would ascend the stage to his lectern where a Biblical passage was read and the school prayer offered before school announcements were given. One morning there was an inordinately long delay before the office door opened. Many boys knew why. Mr Littlejohn had been stopped by a traffic officer for speeding along Mountain Road, a route used each morning by hundreds of boys on their bicycles on their way to school. Hiding was impossible for the embarrassed headmaster!

But even more embarrassing was an announcement Mr Littlejohn made one morning to a hushed assembly. "I am sad to report that it has been brought to my attention by several members of the public that Grammar boys are not standing up for ladies in public conveniences." A sudden silence, then a roar of laughter from the boys who looked over at the masters standing in the shadows at the side of the hall and trying in vain to control their own laughter, which prompted the boys to produce another gale of laughter, as the headmaster himself realised what he had just said, with the double meaning of "standing up" and the verbal slip over "conveyances."

Friday afternoons were taken up with military training, not only marching and rifle exercises and shooting, but also gun routines. I was allocated to a Bofor gun squad and the highlight of the year was putting all our training into action at a coastal firing range.

Grammar provided the ideal preparation for what turned out to be an academic career. I have always been proud to be a "Grammar Old Boy," to have played rugby for all four years for a Grammar team, and to have been a member and badge holder of the school's largest club, the Crusader Union, ably led by Keith Patience, himself a Grammar master. For Crusader boys and others an annual Christmas camp was held on a delightfully isolated island (Ponui) in the Hauraki Gulf near Auckland, an island that was home to sizeable stingrays and wild donkeys. In my final year at Grammar I was a tent leader at Ponui but developed there what turned out to be acute appendicitis and had to be rescued by launch to the mainland where my parents were waiting to take me to hospital. As a result I missed the first two weeks of my two years at Auckland Teachers' College (1957–58).

AUCKLAND TEACHERS' COLLEGE

If a person had gained University Entrance and was at least sixteen years nine months old, he or she could begin study to be a primary (= elementary) school teacher (I was sixteen years ten months!). It was certainly a shock to be in classes with twenty- or thirty-year-olds. Mine had been a relatively sheltered life, so I struggled to cope with the sudden wide range of new ideas. Concerned at what I considered to be pagan ideas being propagated in the child development class, I felt compelled to seek an interview with the Vice-Principal, complaining about ideas that I regarded as "undermining the foundations of our society." He wisely encouraged me to ask penetrating questions of the lecturer, which I did — but to little avail!

Each year I was granted permission to take some lectures at the University and then attend the essential classes missed in alternative sections (I was in the specialist English section each year). This generous provision enabled me to pass Latin I and II and Greek I at the same time as successfully completing College requirements. Thus began a regular pattern of academic life that was not ideal—a pattern of pressing the boundaries and seeking to accomplish two qualifications at once. Corners were regularly cut so that the maximum benefit of various courses was not realized. Courses for honours MA (Auckland) and Diploma in Theology (London) were later undertaken simultaneously, then BD (Otago) and Diploma in Education (Auckland) courses the same way. (One University subsequently began asking all students "Are you registered at any other University?"). Alternatively, a fulltime load of classes was tackled part time. Thus Latin III and Greek II were completed during my first year as a teacher (1958), and nine examinations and a thesis were undertaken in 1962 while teaching at a secondary (high) school. At least I could not be accused of being an under-achiever!

At this time all young men were required to undertake military training for an initial six-week period. Under the influence of a friend, I registered as a conscientious objector in June 1957, only to receive a "Notice of Non-Acceptance for Service on Medical Grounds" (in my case, "Defective Vision") a month later.

Corresponding to the Crusader Union at Grammar was the Evangelical Union at Teachers' College. At Universities and other tertiary institutions throughout New Zealand and worldwide, the EU (now TSCF—Tertiary Students' Christian Fellowship) was a group of Christians on campus who met each week for Christian teaching and fellowship, usually with local ministers or academics as speakers. We also held early morning prayer meetings. In 1958 I was elected the President of the Evangelical Union for that year.

UNIVERSITY OF AUCKLAND

My study at this institution—the leading University in New Zealand—covered the years 1956–64. At the undergraduate level (BA) my majors were Latin and Greek, and at the graduate level (MA and Diploma in Education) Latin with second class honours and educational theory, history, testing, and research. As part of the Diploma I completed a small thesis entitled "Streaming in the Primary School, with special reference to teacher opinion." I had expected to major in French, given my very positive experience in this subject at Grammar. But I wanted to benefit from the renowned Professor Edward Musgrave Blaiklock, Professor of Classics at Auckland, so I enrolled in Latin I. The next year I was told that if I should ever want to progress to an MA in Latin, I would be required to take Greek I. So in year two I enrolled for Latin II and Greek I, thus beginning a lifelong fascination with these two languages.

Affectionately known to his friends as "Ted" and to his students as "EMB" or "the Prof," Professor Blaiklock was internationally acclaimed for his expertise on Euripidean tragedy (his DLitt award was for his "the Male Characters of Euripides") and nationally renowned for his forty-one-year stint as the author of the weekly "Grammaticus" column in the *New Zealand Herald*. But preeminently he was known and loved by multitudes of Christians around the world as a persuasive champion of the Christian faith, an enthralling writer and a mellifluous orator. It was to the memory of Professor Blaiklock (and Professor F. F. Bruce) that I dedicated my commentary on the Greek text of the Gospel of John.

For the Professor's MA students one highlight of the year was the visit for the evening meal to his Titirangi home in the Waitakere Ranges in West Auckland with its panoramic view of the city's sparkling lights. Vehicles had to be left at the bottom of the steep, winding driveway to his home that was slightly below Mount Atkinson, apparently because on one such earlier occasion a car had become stuck on the drive.

```
           THE  UNIVERSITY  OF  AUCKLAND
                (UNIVERSITY OF NEW ZEALAND)


       EXAMINATION FOR HONOURS AND M.A., 1961         No.190


                         LATIN
               Paper (c):  Prose Composition
               (Time allowed:  Three hours)


         As soon as Gallus was invested with the honours of the
      purple, Julian was permitted to breathe the air of freedom, of
      literature, and of paganism.  The crowd of sophists, who were
      attracted by the taste and liberality of their royal pupil, had
      formed a strict alliance between the learning and the religion
      of Greece;  and the poems of Homer, instead of being admired
      as the original productions of human genius, were seriously
      ascribed to the heavenly inspiration of Apollo and the muses.
      The deities of Olympus, as they are painted by the immortal bard,
      imprint themselves on the minds which are the least addicted to
      superstitious credulity.   Our familiar knowledge of their names
      and characters, their forms and attributes, seems to bestow
      on those airy beings a real and substantial existence;  and the
      pleasing enchantment produces an imperfect and momentary assent
      of the imagination to those fables which are the most repugnant
      to our reason and experience.   In the age of Julian every
      circumstance contributed to prolong and fortify the illusion;
      the magnificent temples of Greece and Asia;  the works of those
      artists who had expressed, in painting or in sculpture, the
      divine conceptions of the poet;  the pomp of festivals and
      sacrifices;  the successful arts of divination;  the popular
      traditions of oracles and prodigies;  and the ancient practice of
      two thousand years.  The weakness of polytheism was, in some
      measure, excused by the moderation of its claims;  and the
      devotion of the pagans was not incompatible with the most
      licentious scepticism.

                       - Gibbon:  Decline and Fall of the Roman
                                                 Empire, Ch. 23.
```

UNIVERSITY OF LONDON

Over two years (1960–61) I worked part time on the Diploma in Theology from the University of London. It had the distinct advantage of exams held in June in keeping with the northern hemisphere, and a special paper on the Vulgate that suited my specialty in Latin. Strange it was to receive the Pass List that included the solitary NZ entry, "New Zealand (Auckland) * 4922. Harris, Murray James . . . Private study."

UNIVERSITY OF OTAGO

At that time the only institution in New Zealand that offered graduate Bachelor of Divinity courses in Biblical studies and theology was the Presbyterian Knox College in Dunedin whose faculty simultaneously served in the Faculty of Theology of the University of Otago. Lectures given at Knox effectively served as the basis for the university exams—which was fine for internal students but a challenge for extra-mural students. So, in preparing for church history exams I sought to discover what particular topics formed the focus of Knox College lectures which were likely to be reflected in the BD exams! My completion of this degree was postponed when we set off for the University of Manchester in August 1965.

During these years of study at the Universities of Auckland, London and Otago, my days were exceptionally full: teaching 9am–4pm, often lectures 5pm–8pm, study 9pm onwards, and the exhilarating diversion of courting my future wife, Jennifer, from 1961–63. One feels weak at the knees to recall those busy days. Sometimes I would meet Jennifer when she came off nursing duty at Middlemore Hospital at 11pm or take her there to begin the midnight shift. In such cases, after a full day of teaching and study I would often drive with my window wide open to ensure I stayed awake!

UNIVERSITY OF MANCHESTER

Some may be mystified why I chose Manchester over, say, Oxford or Cambridge or Harvard for my advanced Biblical studies. When I was contemplating overseas study I consulted two well-known and highly respected Christian leaders in Auckland—Rev Alan Burrow, then Principal of the Bible College of New Zealand, and Rev Graham Miller, Presbyterian minister in Papakura. Both recommended Professor Frederick Fyvie Bruce, Rylands Professor of Biblical Criticism and Exegesis in the University of Manchester (although Mr Burrow naturally also mentioned his alma mater, Dallas Theological Seminary!).

It is sometimes said of the Dutch Reformer Erasmus that he "laid the egg that Luther hatched." Of Professor Bruce it could be said that he laid the egg which evangelical scholarship worldwide has now hatched. Seventy years ago, first-rate evangelical biblical scholarship was scarcely visible in any part of the globe; today it is flourishing throughout the English-speaking world. We cannot account for this monumental reversal without recognizing the worldwide influence of British evangelicalism and in particular the pioneering leadership of F.F. Bruce. He was intimately involved in the discussions and plans that led to the establishment of a residential library for biblical research (Tyndale House) in Cambridge (1944) and the creation of the Tyndale Fellowship for Biblical Research (1945), both actions being aimed at removing the stigma of unscholarliness and obscurantism from evangelicalism by fostering biblical research in a spirit of loyalty to the historic Christian faith. An indication of this resurgence of evangelicalism may be seen in the large number of evangelical authors involved in the very recent *New Cambridge Bible Commentary* series.

Most scholars, whatever their theological stripe, would call F. F. Bruce the most distinguished evangelical Biblical scholar of the 20th century, and not a few would declare him to be the most notable Biblical scholar of any theological persuasion during last century. He was one of only two persons (Matthew Black was the other) ever to be elected to the presidency of both the Society for Old Testament Study (1965) and the Society for New Testament Study (1975), the premier international societies of Biblical scholars. After all, he held the Rylands Chair of *Biblical* Criticism and Exegesis. Although most of his writing and commentaries are on the New Testament, he wrote three short monographs on the Dead Sea Scrolls, documents that are at the intersection of the Testaments; he delivered Tyndale Lectures on both the Old Testament (1947) and the New (1941, 1968); he authored what amounts to an introduction to the Bible, *The Books and the Parchments*, and a comprehensive investigation of *The Canon of Scripture*; and he was editor of the *Palestine Exploration Quarterly* for fourteen years (1957–71).

I was privileged to write the chapter on Professor Bruce in *Bible Interpreters of the Twentieth Century. A Selection of Evangelical Voices* (ed. Walter A. Elwell and J. D. Weaver; Baker: Grand Rapids, 1999, 216–27). And a fellow PhD student, Donald A. Hagner, and I edited and contributed to *Pauline Studies. Essays Presented to Professor F. F. Bruce on his 70th birthday* (Exeter: Paternoster, 1980). This was the second set of essays written in Bruce's honour. The earlier collection, *Apostolic History and the Gospel:*

EDUCATION

Biblical and Historical Essays Presented to F. F. Bruce on his 60th Birthday (eds. W. W. Gasque and R. P. Martin; Exeter: Paternoster; Grand Rapids: Eerdmans), appeared in 1970.

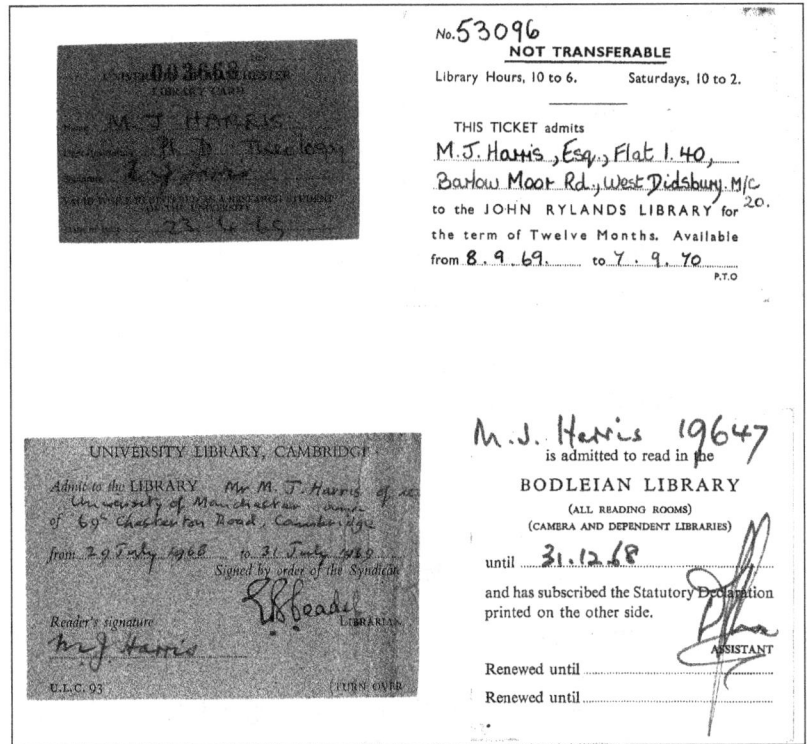

Library cards for Manchester and Oxford

Little wonder, then, that I duly applied to be admitted to the MA programme in Biblical studies in Manchester. Our initial intention was to return to New Zealand when the one- or two-year course was over. It involved two exam papers, one on the Greek texts of Matthew and 2 Corinthians, the other on New Testament historical and critical issues, along with a thirty-to-forty-thousand-word thesis. As for my choice of a research topic, I had always had a special interest in Paul's view of death, resurrection and immortality. A monograph had recently been published on 1 Corinthians 15 so I decided to write on "The Exegesis of 2 Corinthians 5:1–10, and Its Place in Pauline Eschatology." When the research was finally completed in 1970 (as a much longer PhD thesis), it met with the approval of the two examiners, Professor Bruce himself and Professor C. D. F. Moule, Lady Margaret's

Professor in the University of Cambridge. In his own autobiography, *In Retrospect: Remembrance of Things Past* (revised posthumous ed.; Baker: Grand Rapids, 1993), Professor Bruce kindly refers to my work "which his Cambridge external examiner pronounced to be the best Ph.D. thesis he had ever read." (That examiner had himself written on the problems of 2 Corinthians 5:1–10, and Dr Harris had argued against him, but that enhanced, rather than diminished, his appreciation of the thesis)" (233). In that same volume Bruce observes "I can think of no better foundation than a classical education for the professional cultivation of biblical studies" (145).

So then, this timid Kiwi lad from "Down Under" had become, for better or worse, the product of four Universities—two in New Zealand, and two in the UK. He always was proud of his purely University pedigree, and perversely proud of the fact that he had never darkened the door of a theological institution and so could not be branded or dismissed as a Calvinist or an Arminian, a fundamentalist or a liberal, as a result of particular theological indoctrination.

LIFE IN MANCHESTER

Both Jennifer's nursing qualification and my teaching qualification were immediately recognised in England. In our second year in Manchester Jennifer nursed at Nathan House, the private wing of Christie Hospital & Holt Radium Institute that specialised in cancer treatment. Not only England's leading cancer surgeons but also wealthy or influential patients from around the world could be found at this hospital. For example, Jennifer received an official invitation to attend the Installation Ceremony of Chief Emanuel Okusanya Okunowo, M.B.E., as Lay-President of the African Church (Inc.) in Lagos, Western Nigeria.

At the end of my first academic year I did some relieving teaching at Collyhurst co-ed "Secondary Modern" School, a church—related school situated in a low socio-economic area of north Manchester. The children arrived at school without lunch, books or writing implements, so everything had to be supplied. At interval time after my first class, when ballpoint pens had been collected, it became clear that we were short of about six or seven pens. So I assured them that no one was leaving until we had a full count. A long silence. What would he do to those who confessed? When they realised that I was serious, first one then another sheepishly surrendered their loot. Another interval. Then further surrenders, as the reality of facing the frustrated wrath of their classmates sank in. It was also humorous to watch their creative and stealthy escapades during the compulsory chapel attendance—"out of sight, out of mind."

For exercise and enjoyment I frequented the university squash courts. At the height of my fitness, if my partner failed to turn up, I could play myself for thirty minutes. For relaxation we sometimes attended performances in the Town Hall of the Halle Orchestra conducted by Sir John Barbirolli. For the six months we owned a car (a trade-in from a vehicle dealer in Park Lane, London—of Monopoly fame), we attended Bramhall Chapel in the southern suburbs, then we attended Ivy Cottage Church, one of the Association of Independent Churches, situated almost directly opposite our apartment. Once a month, research students in the Faculty of Theology met informally for fellowship and Bible study. During term time formal seminars were held weekly within the Faculty when visiting scholars or occasionally one of our group of student researchers read a paper that prompted questions and vigorous discussion.

Among my many recollections of our four Manchester years (1965–67, 1969–70), three experiences remain emblazoned on my memory.

In the UK major exams are held at the end of the academic year. As indicated earlier, one part of the requirements for the MA degree were two crucial exams (or "papers", as they are called), the first of which was on the Greek text of Matthew and 2 Corinthians. Leaving very adequate time for an unhurried arrival at the special examination rooms before 9:45am, I caught my regular number 32 Didsbury bus to the University. But alas! Halfway on the twenty-five-minute journey the crowded bus that had standing room only, came to an abrupt and ominous halt outside the Memorial Gardens, and would not restart. What was I to do? Walk—or run?—the remaining distance, but would that get me there on time? Most passengers seemed not unduly concerned; half an hour late to work or for shopping was not the end of the world. But it was vastly different for my world: the reason for our coming to the UK, and my whole future, seemed to be at stake. After a prolonged delay, during which my concern steadily mounted, a replacement vehicle arrived—and my Kiwi reticence and politeness suddenly deserted me as we all jostled for a seat. I did arrive just in time to begin the crucial exam.

But the story does not end there. Once the second exam was over two days later, I began teaching at Collyhurst Secondary Modern School, as described earlier. Weeks passed and there was no word about exam results. I was unsure how MA students were informed of their results. Was it a case of "No news is good news"? After some time I plucked up courage to contact Professor Bruce who kindly sent a letter indicating I had passed and that included the report of the external examiner (Dr A. J. B. Higgins of the University of Leeds) regarding that first exam: "Harris is extraordinarily good, indeed brilliant, with excellent idiomatic translations and first-rate comments revealing knowledge of the views of a number of scholars on a variety of exegetical problems. It was a pleasure to read his work, which fully deserves the very high mark of 90%."

The second indelible memory concerns a special letter I was asked to collect from the local post office. I vividly remember opening it at the intersection of Palatine and Barlow Moor Roads. It was from a person and place totally unknown to me, being an offer from Dean Kenneth S. Kantzer of an eleven-month teaching position as a Visiting Professor at Trinity Evangelical Divinity School for the academic year 1967–68 for the princely sum of $8000 US dollars. (We were currently paying twenty-seven pounds per month for the rental of our Manchester flat!). It turned out that one of our first-year colleagues, Paul Leonard, on returning to Trinity after one year of research at Manchester, had informed Kantzer of our situation and suggested that an approach be made to me to enable him to spend another year of PhD research in the UK. Little did Paul and the Dean know that in the divine providence the direction of our lives would be changed for ever by that letter—a total of nineteen years spent in the USA, teaching at Trinity. Is this possibly an illustration of the axiom, "Big doors swing on small hinges"?

After our initial year at Manchester towards the MA degree, we had been transferred into the PhD programme, also in the Faculty of Arts (not Theology), but at the time the letter arrived we were altogether uncertain how we would finance the remaining two or three years of the programme. In the event, during those eleven months in the USA we were able to save more than we could have earned in New Zealand during the same period! Quite apart from and before any action on our part, God was providing for our need.

The third unforgettable episode occurred over two days at the end of our fourth year at Manchester. Usually the interval between the submission of one's thesis and the oral exam based on it is about four weeks. But, as it happened, both of my examiners, Professors Bruce and Moule, had been scheduled for US lecturing tours long before my thesis was submitted so there was an unexpected eleven-week delay before the oral. Jennifer had returned to New Zealand on January 6 to be with her ailing mother. My thesis defence took place on the morning of May 22. It had become a custom for the candidate to call Professor Bruce on the evening of the oral to hear the official outcome, which I duly did. But Bruce had already kindly reassured me immediately before the oral that he and Moule had approved the thesis and indicated that Moule simply wanted to discuss some points of special interest (which he did, jotting down some notes about a German tome he had not yet read—P. Hoffmann, *Die Toten in Christus*). So I departed for New Zealand the next day via London. As we crossed the English Channel in perfect weather, I clearly remember looking down on dozens of ships moving across the Channel like ants on a pavement, as I recalled Professor Moule's reaction to my thesis conveyed to me by my mentor (see earlier), reflected on "Mission Accomplished" after four years in Manchester, and anticipated my upcoming reunion with Jennifer after almost five months apart, also knowing that a temporary position was awaiting me at my former secondary school (Glendowie College). What more could a person want?

While waiting for my oral exam, I applied for the only two positions available. One was at Massey University in New Zealand in the general field of Religious Studies. My specialty was not in the philosophy or psychology of religion or comparative religion, so I was not surprised that I was unsuccessful. The other was a New Testament position in the Faculty of Theology in the University of Manchester! I applied and then survived an interview but the position understandably went to a Britisher who had been teaching in an African University for several years. The other two interviewees were older men, parish ministers with doctorates. Here I was, a youngster not yet with a Manchester PhD. But time and maturity would bring change.

3

Teaching Career (I)

AUCKLAND TEACHERS' COLLEGE (1956–57)

AN ESSENTIAL PART OF our training was our "sections," when for a month we were under the supervision of a senior teacher at various schools, observing teacher practice, interacting with pupils, and occasionally ourselves teaching while our mentor critiqued our performance. This exposure to varying teaching techniques and different school traditions proved invaluable. My most memorable "section" was at Auckland's War Memorial Museum (on the steps of which I later proposed to Jennifer in 1961!). Classes of children would be bussed to the museum from surrounding schools and we were responsible to guide the youngsters through the various exhibits as they recorded answers to written questions and drew pictures or diagrams of their own. Since the museum boasts the world's largest collections of Maori and Polynesian artefacts, there was a natural focus on indigenous history and customs. Not infrequently one's first teaching placement was at a school to which we had been introduced on a "section."

MEADOWBANK PRIMARY SCHOOL (1958)

One's first teaching assignment was called the Probationary Assistant (PA) year, with the school's headmaster or headmistress acting as supervisor, advisor and encourager. As an eighteen-year old I was entrusted with thirty-two eight-year olds! This would never happen today. Since PAs were not permitted to use corporal punishment, one quickly learned alternative methods of reward and punishment. My most effective technique was to threaten a mischief-maker with the prospect of spending a day in a lower class. Rarely did this actually happen, such would be the loss of "face" with classmates through this demotion. One particular pleasure in my PA year was having my prospective mother-in-law, Jessie McCracken, as the "Bible in Schools" teacher for my class. During this half-hour away from their classes, teachers usually had a meeting with the headmaster—unless pupils proved too unruly for the visiting teacher to cope.

I well remember the afternoon when the "senior classes" of seven to ten-year-olds, arranged in foursomes on the large playground, were being instructed by the headmaster on the finer points of "square dancing." He was a sturdy man, having excelled in cricket as a fast bowler. When a wayward boy in the far distance was seen to be tossing a tennis ball around his group, the headmaster bellowed out, "Bring that ball here!" On receiving it, he wound up his massive frame and hurled the ball over a distant row of trees, evidently forgetting that this was a light tennis ball, not a cricket ball. The "follow-through" was awe-inspiring as he felt flat on his face. The senior mistress hastened up, "Are you alright, Cederick?" The children could scarcely contain their glee but were too frightened to express it, remembering the headmaster's devastating skill with the strap.

People are now often amazed that an eighteen-year-old who began his teaching career with eight-year olds in little New Zealand finished that career as an Emeritus Professor of a graduate School of an American University, travelling via the Directorship of a research library in Cambridge and being a faculty member of the University there.

GLENDOWIE PRIMARY SCHOOL (1959–60)

During the first of the two years at this school I taught a "Standard 4" class of thirty-seven ten-year-olds. Education in New Zealand has always been "free, compulsory, and secular." But, perhaps in recognition of our nation's Christian roots, there has been provision in primary (= elementary) schools for "Bible in Schools" for one half-hour period at the beginning of the day once a week. Technically, the school day begins at 9:30am on those days. On a voluntary basis local Christians, whether parents or church personnel, introduce youngsters to Bible stories and Christian values in a creative manner. Normally staff meetings are held at this time, but I was released by our headmaster to conduct these special classes with my own class. So one minute the children may be illustrating a Bible story or praying together, and the next minute undertaking a spelling or arithmetic test! From my perspective this was "Christianity in action" and an ideal way for children to gain a holistic view of the Faith.

I will never forget one hilarious episode. On one occasion as I was carrying out the required lunchtime "playground duty," I noticed that a small bevvy of boys was systematically following me at a discreet distance and quickly refocussing their gaze when I turned around. On returning to the classroom at the end of the lunchtime break, I found the blackboard duster and chalk strategically placed on the floor at the base of the blackboard. I later discovered that a sizeable split had occurred in the seam of my trousers and these rascals hoped that they would become witnesses of a massive cleavage! But they had done nothing wrong in following me—and the duster and chalk has simply fallen off the ledge! I said or did nothing, of course—except laugh privately and have the trousers repaired.

At this age level (and at this time) teachers were required to teach the whole range of relevant subjects, not simply the traditional "reading, writing and arithmetic." I thoroughly enjoyed conducting PE (physical education) classes, incorporating a wide range of competitive races as well as the required exercises. And I coped with "music" by having a desk harp to ensure the right pitch for class singing. But since "science" had never been my forte, I struggled to hold the students' attention, unless we were investigating God's handiwork in nature or the stars and planets.

During my second year my "Form 1 & 2" class of thirty-two eleven—and twelve-year-olds afforded the challenge of teaching two different age groups with different syllabi, although the one-year difference in age was insignificant when they were doing art work or when I was reading English classics to them, such as "David Copperfield." My coaching skills were put to the test when I was responsible for junior girls' basketball. Every second year a school was subject to an inspectorial visit, and teachers were "graded" on teaching ability and progress. A significant increase in "grade" could lead to a promotion and with it a higher salary.

GLENDOWIE COLLEGE (1962–65, 1970)

Mine was an ideal introduction to secondary school teaching. The year began with a cricket match between the male teachers and a carefully selected boys' team. Evidently I made a lasting positive impression on all—whether boys or girls—when I hit a massive "six" and the ball was irretrievably lost in the undergrowth. This man is to be respected!

The college was in its second year and was adding an additional intake of students each year, so it was an ideal situation for positive traditions to be built up. Our principal was Lyn Adams, a fine Christian gentleman who carefully crafted his own prayers that he offered each morning at the school assembly—undoubtedly a practice unparalleled among principals in our secular schools. He also warmly encouraged the Crusader Union that enjoyed the support of no fewer than five of us teachers. The warm collegiality of the staff was reflected in the generous hospitality of Mr and Mrs Adams in the annual end-of-year function in their home. When Jennifer experienced her serious illness at the end of 1970, the first bouquet of flowers to arrive at the hospital came from Lyn Adams.

My teaching subjects were English, social studies, and especially Latin for years one to four. It did not take long for the first-year Latin class to overhear others repeating the ditty, "Latin's a dead language, Dead as dead can be, First it killed the Romans, Now it's killing me." My extra-curricula responsibilities were twofold: organising the free textbook scheme funded by the government, and coaching the two boys' tennis teams that played on Saturdays.

I was invited to offer the dedicatory prayer at the official Opening Ceremony of the college a year after it was established in 1961. The ceremony was attended by various dignatories including the Mayor of Auckland and the Member of Parliament for Tamaki at that time, Robert Muldoon, who later became Prime Minister of New Zealand.

On my return to New Zealand from the UK at the end of May in 1970, I taught again at the College before taking up a permanent position at Trinity in March 1971. My Glendowie colleagues jokingly said, "Now there's a doctor in the house!" The close proximity of the College to St Andrew's Hospital meant I could walk to visit my mother there each lunch hour. She passed away in August of the following year when we were back in the USA.

4

Teaching Career (II)

IN CHAPTER 2 (p. 21) I indicated how I first came to be invited to teach at Trinity Evangelical Divinity School (hereafter TEDS). We can trace the ultimate roots of TEDS to a Bible study course organised by the Swedish Evangelical Free Church in Chicago in 1897. But it was in 1963 that TEDS was formally created at the instigation of Dr Kenneth S. Kantzer and came to be located in Deerfield, Illinois, on the north side of Chicago. Dr Kantzer viewed TEDS as a "love gift" from the Evangelical Free Church of America to the local and global church. Its faculty members have always represented diverse theological traditions and cultural backgrounds but have shared a commitment to evangelical Christianity. TEDS is now part of Trinity International University and has over one thousand two hundred graduate students including more than one hundred and fifty in various PhD programs. Immediately before our return to New Zealand in 1997 I was privileged to be the speaker at the one hundredth Annual Commencement ceremony, choosing as my topic, "Slave of Christ: the Christian's Consummate Privilege."

All of my teaching at TEDS over the years has been in the field of NT studies, involving subjects such as Beginning Greek, Greek Exegesis, Greek grammar, Acts and the Pauline epistles, and the Corinthian correspondence, or the history of NT Theology for doctoral students. My only incursion into the Old Testament was a course on the Septuagint (LXX), the Old Testament in Greek.

Teaching Career (II)

1967–68 AT TRINITY EVANGELICAL DIVINITY SCHOOL (TEDS)

The expected eleven-month US adventure turned out to be a full year because I unexpectedly received an invitation to give some Biblical and church history lectures at Winona Lake School of Theology when the designated lecturer suddenly became ill. This invitation arrived in a strange way. I was at a special late-night sitting in a dentist's chair in Manchester to receive a gold filling before our upcoming departure for the US, when the nurse came in bearing an urgent message that had just arrived, asking me to phone Warsaw as soon as possible. I thought, "Why on earth did someone called *Dr Hoffmann* in *Poland* want me to telephone him immediately? I had not ever had dubious Polish dealings—or in fact anything to do with Poland. And in any case, how did the secret police in Poland know that right then I was at a particular dentist's in Manchester?" In reality it was a call from a Dr John *Huffman* of the School of Theology at Winona Lake near Warsaw, *Indiana*, and it was my wife who was the informant as to my whereabouts. We gladly accepted the invitation and so departed in mid-July instead of the expected mid-August.

My first TEDS course was the Summer Beginning Greek course that students who had not included Greek in their undergraduate course could take in preparation for the Greek Exegesis courses that were a required part of the MDiv. We met for four hours a day, six days a week, for six weeks. The course was regularly called "Suicide Greek," students being reassured by others that if they survived that gruelling schedule, nothing else that Trinity required would induce suicide. I preferred to remind them that they would now be able to relax during the first six weeks in heaven while others toiled to acquire the heavenly language! I also had to remind them, this time seriously, that no language can be mastered in six weeks and that a little knowledge can be a very dangerous thing. At the end of the six weeks they would not be qualified to improve the English translations of the Greek NT or correct technical commentaries based on the Greek text.

We jokingly say that during this first year, we saw nothing of the USA. We lived in the windowless basement of a home in Zion (!), we attended a small church that met in the basement of a funeral home, and my windowless office at TEDS was in the centre of a classroom complex. For all that, ours was an ideal introduction to the warm friendliness and positive outlook that characterize the vast majority of Americans.

Before I Forget

1971–78 AT TEDS

In these early days at TEDS my teaching regularly involved the summer "Suicide Greek" class mentioned earlier. The 1971 version was memorable for two reasons. At the end I was presented with a card of appreciation that bore the signatures of all the students and also this observation: "Sometimes I forget you have a right to have moods, too. *Indicative, SUBJUNCTIVE, IMPERATIVE, Infinitive, Optative.*" Moreover, one of my students then was W. Bingham Hunter, who later became Dean at TEDS!

If people were mystified why I always taught several Summer School classes, the reason was simple. It generated extra finance for mortgage repayments, and I have always enjoyed interaction with students who are keen to learn. In 1975, while Jennifer and our infant son Oliver were in New Zealand visiting family, I set a questionable record by teaching three summer classes at once—Beginning Greek for four hours in the morning, Greek Exegesis for three hours in the afternoon, and Acts and the Pauline epistles for three hours in the evening. The Registrar subsequently barred such foolishness! But my teaching techniques at least throughout the regular school year must not have seemed too objectional, for in 1973 I was voted "Man of the Year" by the editors of the student magazine, the *Scribe*.

During this period I was privileged to take two sabbaticals, each being one term or quarter plus the summer break, giving six months. The first was spent in New Zealand where we hoped to be able to adopt a child. Back in 1970, after our return from Manchester, Jennifer contracted toxaemia (or pre-eclampsia as it is now often called), a serious complication of pregnancy marked by an accumulation of water in the tissues, high blood pressure and headaches, and sudden weight gain. If symptoms persist, a kind of epilepsy (eclampsia) occurs that can prove fatal to both mother and child. To prevent this, a termination of the pregnancy is sometimes necessary. Since Jennifer had developed acute toxaemia, the surgeon reluctantly recommended termination and discouraged any further pregnancy. I had spoken that Sunday morning at our church on the topic of the love of God; by that evening I received news that while Jennifer's life had been spared, our infant daughter (whom we later named Susan) had survived only six hours fifty minutes. Here was the love of God at work—sparing one life and taking another back to himself. Jennifer's fulminating toxaemia and subsequent six months of double vision may have been (so doctors told us) the first symptoms of the multiple sclerosis later diagnosed (see below, chapter 12, p. 89).

Teaching Career (II)

All this prompted our eagerness to enquire about an adoption when back in New Zealand in 1973. We completed all the necessary preliminaries, including the required parenting course. To our great delight, those six months enabled us to adopt Oliver James at birth, complete the legal aspects of adoption, and secure his immigration rights.

My second sabbatical at the end of 1976 proved equally exciting for the three of us but in a totally different way. We flew to Athens which enabled me to spend two days in Old Corinth, visiting the archaeological sites and climbing the Acrocorinth. When I was at the bustling Athens airport, waiting for a bus to rejoin Jennifer in the city, I blithely added my luggage to an accumulating pile alongside a bus marked "To Athens" that soon took off. A few minutes later, a woman stood authoritatively at the front on the bus and began to count. "Un, deux, trois, quatre, ..." I had unknowingly attached myself to a French tour party, and they soon focussed their gaze of the extra passenger. However, they kindly delivered me to a spot near our hotel. Oliver was glad to see Daddy again! But there was more excitement to come.  Next day, thirty minutes into our flight to Tel Aviv the captain announced that we would be returning to Athens. A fog had descended on Tel Aviv airport that made landing impossible, we were told. Or, in fact, had there been a security alert somewhere in Israel? But return to Athens we did, until 5am the following day.

Some months previously we had arranged to be housed in the Old City in the quarters of the American Institute of Holy Land Studies (as it was then called) near David's Tomb. My only responsibility was to be chaplain during the visits to Israel of student groups from various American undergraduate colleges. During those three months in Israel I was able to use the library facilities of the renowned École Biblique, and to attend lectures by visiting Israeli scholars on Jewish history, Jews in America, and Jew-Arab relations. And all three of us accompanied the students who were studying at the Institute on their field trips, some of two or three days, to Greater Jerusalem, Samaria, the Negev (including Masada and Qumran), Galilee, Philistia, and the Mar Saba Monastery. During one tour we visited the probable site of young David's encounter with Goliath and gathered stones from the nearby brook to remind us of David's ammunition. Our bus driver was Feiss, a burly giant who had once driven tanks, so we ventured into places that were off the beaten track. At this location, to dramatize the moment, he held little Oliver on his upturned palm above his head while everyone took camera shots. So enthusiastic was I about the benefits and pleasure of visiting Israel that on returning to Trinity I

Jennifer and Oliver catch a taxi in Jerusalem

Teaching Career (II)

encouraged the formation of annual tours to Israel for groups of TEDS students—a successful innovation.

During the seven years being reviewed we lived in four different homes. The first, in Highland Park, we rented, then with great excitement we purchased our first home that was situated in Wildwood. Then followed homes in Lake Forest and Highland Park. The reason for the regular shifts? Each was nearer to Trinity, and each was more expensive than the last, because when salary was being determined, "ministers of the gospel" (including teachers at a church-affiliated institution) could specify as a tax deductible amount a housing allowance made up of mortgage payments. In addition, these same payments were also deductible under "Itemised Deductions" in tax returns in what was called the "double dip," a taxation anomaly that was tested in court more than once. This whole arrangement was modelled on the situation for people in the military. Moreover, tax on gains made through the sale of residences could be indefinitely postponed. And with letters of commendation from the elders of Tamaki Bible Chapel in Auckland and the elders of Queen Edith Chapel in Cambridge, I was exempt from self-employment tax. So we were simply capitalizing on established taxation provisions, and in so doing were being shrewd as "the people of the light" (Luke 16:8).

On one occasion in Lake Forest, during a Chicago sub-zero winter, the lightly-clad Jennifer dashed out to get the mail, but on returning to the front door discovered it was firmly shut and locked. The three-year-old Oliver had decided to keep the cold out (!) so had obligingly closed the door and was passing the time until Jennifer returned by carefully letting tissues float downstairs one by one from our upstairs balcony. Our neighbours came to the rescue, calling the fire brigade to check whether any windows might be partially open to enable entry. To everyone's relief an upstairs bathroom window at the rear was slightly ajar so an officer was able to prise it open and scramble in.

It is a source of some embarrassment to record that in this period of seven years I received several offers of alternative academic positions. During the 25th Annual Meeting of the Evangelical Theological Society in December 1973, a meeting that brought together a wide array of evangelical scholars, I was interviewed about a possible post at Gordon-Conwell Theological Seminary in Wenham, Massachusetts (an approach repeated by letter in October, 1976). But I had just been promoted to a full professorship at Trinity! Then, after prolonged correspondence with Dr James

M. Houston, Principal of Regent College, I visited Vancouver in 1975 for interviews. Dr Houston's dream was that after a period at Regent I might be able to help establish a comparable college in New Zealand. But the inordinately high cost of housing in Vancouver at the time, the recency of our return to Trinity, and gentle pressure from Dean Kantzer led us to decline the offer. As it happened, at about the same time the General Secretary of the Tertiary Students' Christian Fellowship in New Zealand enquired about the possibility of my spending a year in 1977 or 1978 in a lecture tour with a view to the creation of a "Christian Graduate Study Community" in Christchurch.

Jennifer's father, Jack McCracken, died suddenly in October 1977, and in a strange set of circumstances we were able to visit "home" briefly, be with Jennifer's mother, and take part in the funeral. We will always be glad that this unexpectedly proved possible because we could not be present at the funeral of Jennifer's mother or at my parents' funerals. These two weeks gave us time to evaluate carefully two opportunities that had arisen in New Zealand. One was the chaplaincy at the Maclaurin Chapel of the University of Auckland. An interview was hurriedly arranged, but in spite of the attraction of serving students at my alma mater, particularly in the field of pre-marital counselling, the prospect of conducting fifty or more marriages a year for five or even eight years seemed difficult to square with my training and plans for future teaching and writing. On the other hand, the offer of a permanent post in New Testament studies at the Bible College of New Zealand in Auckland seemed admirably to suit my background and probable future. It was the only comparable position anywhere in New Zealand, and since our plan had always been to return home for permanent service, we believed this was the right time to follow through with our longstanding goal. So on November 23, 1977, with very mixed emotions I submitted my resignation to Dean Kantzer at Trinity, effective in June of 1978.

It has always been a source of great amusement to our Kiwi friends that my final contribution (as I thought it was at the time) to life in the USA was to conduct a seminar for my TEDS colleagues on US taxation as it affected theological teachers! At a farewell function for Jennifer, put on by the Trinity faculty wives in one of their homes, she was escorted to a large upstairs bedroom where they had set out on display all of the handwork that Jennifer had made for them—such as table runners, decorative hangings, Christmas decorations, and mementos. Little wonder, then, that in one of my books dedicated to her I spoke of her as a modern-day Dorcas (see Acts 9:36–39).

Mention should be made of two sightseeing tours we undertook during these first eight years in the USA. In June and July in 1972 we travelled through fourteen states to the south and east of Chicago, camping all the way. Highlights included visits to the Cowboy Hall of Fame in Oklahoma, Six Flags Over Texas, the final night of Explo '72 (organized by Campus Crusade for Christ) in the Cotton Bowl (75,000 seating capacity) with closed circuit TV in the adjoining Coliseum and Billy Graham preaching, NASA in Houston, the Old Quarter of New Orleans, and the Great Smoky Mountains National Park.

In the first part of our return to New Zealand in 1978 we travelled west by car from Chicago to Los Angeles. Not surprisingly, this tour included the Garden of the Gods and the (literally) breath-taking cog railway up to Pike's Peak (14,110 feet) in Colorado, the world's highest suspension bridge in Royal Gorge Park, Bryce and Zion Canyons, the South Rim of the Grand Canyon (an awe-inspiring, humbling experience), Disneyland (Oliver was mesmerised by the Electrical Parade), Marineland, and Hollywood.

5

Teaching Career (III)

1986–97 AT TEDS

OUR FIVE YEARS IN Cambridge (1981–86, see chapter 7) proved both enjoyable and rewarding. Study cubicles in the Tyndale House Library and extension were fully booked and accommodation above the Library and in the House itself was always in demand. Under God's good hand and with the generous support of Christians in the UK, the USA and elsewhere, the venture that had begun in 1944 was flourishing in the 1980s. But as had happened before, just when we felt happily settled and believed that Auckland (NZ) or Cambridge (UK) would be the city of our retirement, an unexpected opportunity presented itself. TEDS had decided to develop a PhD programme in theological studies (subsequently accredited by the Association of Theological Schools) and the School was needing suitable personnel to pioneer its establishment. Extended communication from the Academic Dean at the time, Dr Walter Kaiser, and a visit to Cambridge by the President, Dr Ken Meyer, forced us to consider seriously their offer to us to return to TEDS in a somewhat different role. Given my reluctance to assume new administrative responsibilities, I was given the luxury of stating the conditions of a return: I would never be the Director of the PhD programme; my teaching responsibilities would involve two not the usual three classes per quarter; my mentoring of master's theses as first reader would be limited to three active theses at any one time; I would be responsible for only one doctoral seminar per year; and I would have additional secretarial and graduate assistant help, to enable me to have more time for research and writing than had been the case at Tyndale House. With these provisions securely in place, I agreed to assume a new endowed Chair as Professor of New Testament Exegesis and Theology, beginning in the Fall Quarter of 1986.

This decision was made after a long period of thought, consultation and prayer, including a brief visit to the USA by Jennifer and myself. We considered that it would probably not be in the best interest of Tyndale House for there to be a single incumbent of the Wardenship for twenty years, and that if there was to be a move before retirement it would be less of an upheaval for the children when they were younger. Also, a return to the USA would mean we were closer to New Zealand! In all this we were being reminded that the Lord of the Vineyard reserves the right to move his workers around his plantation as he chooses. Confirmation of the rightness of the move came on two fronts. We gained a cash sale of our Cambridge property to the renter, along with all the furniture. (We had lived in the Warden's Lodge at Tyndale House). Then, with an unexpected travel grant from Trinity that enabled a "house-hunting" visit to the US and with the efficient help of TEDS friends, we were able to purchase a suitable property in Lake Forest only ten minutes' drive from Trinity—and we moved in directly from the airport! Both of these real estate ventures took place without the cost of agents.

For anyone teaching at the tertiary level, there is no experience more intellectually stimulating and rewarding than conducting a PhD seminar. Both teacher and students are operating at their highest level and (ideally) benefitting from the cut and thrust of Socratic dialogue. Here scholars are in the making. As I look down class lists, again and again I see the names of people now holding prominent academic positions. Little wonder, then, at my pleasure once TEDS began its PhD programme in theological studies in leading such seminars on "The History of New Testament Theologies" and "The Use of *Theos* as a Christological Title." The latter topic led to the publication of *Jesus as God* (1992), while the former prompted me to outline a detailed book on New Testament theology (that I will never write).

> **CERTIFICATE OF COPYRIGHT REGISTRATION**
>
> This certificate, issued under the seal of the Copyright Office in accordance with the provisions of section 410(a) of title 17, United States Code, attests that copyright registration has been made for the work identified below. The information in this certificate has been made a part of the Copyright Office records.
>
> REGISTER OF COPYRIGHTS, United States of America
>
> **FORM TX** — UNITED STATES COPYRIGHT OFFICE
> REGISTRATION NUMBER: TXU 436 109
> EFFECTIVE DATE OF REGISTRATION: 9 / 24 / 90
>
> 1. **TITLE OF THIS WORK:** RULES and BOARD for the GAME of "SMUDGE"
>   PREVIOUS OR ALTERNATIVE TITLES: None
>
> 2. **NAME OF AUTHOR:** MURRAY JAMES HARRIS
>   DATES OF BIRTH AND DEATH: 3-19-39 / N/A
>   AUTHOR'S NATIONALITY OR DOMICILE: Domiciled in U.S.A.
>   NATURE OF AUTHORSHIP: Entire text and artwork
>
> 3. **YEAR IN WHICH CREATION OF THIS WORK WAS COMPLETED:** 1990
>
> 4. **COPYRIGHT CLAIMANT(S):** MURRAY JAMES HARRIS, 26996 N. Longwood Drive, Lake Forest, IL 60045
>   APPLICATION RECEIVED: SEP 24 1990
>   ONE DEPOSIT RECEIVED: SEP 24 1990

This board game was copyrighted (along with the rules) in the US Copyright Office of the Library of Congress

Doctor of Ministry (DMin) seminars were enjoyable for a different reason. Here were seasoned pastors wanting to deepen their competence in specific practical fields. I remember a 1988 DMin TEDS extension course in Kristiansand on the south coast of Norway when we investigated Paul's pastoral techniques especially as seen in his Corinthian correspondence. (Locals proudly told me that there was a higher percentage of Christians per square mile in this region than anywhere else in the world!). I had already enjoyed a visit to Norway to attend the 40th meeting of the Society for New Testament Studies in Trondheim in 1986. (The SNTS is the premier international society of New Testament scholars, of which I became an elected member in 1984).

The second half of 1993 proved to be one of my most memorable sabbaticals. In June of that year, while on tour in New Zealand and Australia, I had the opportunity to deliver three widely advertised University lectures. The first was at Macquarie University's Society for the Study of Early Christianity on the topic "The Use of *Theos* as a Christological Title in the New Testament" that was based on my book *Jesus as God* (1992). The second was held at the University of Auckland and sponsored by the Bible College of New Zealand. The three questions discussed were "Did Jesus Exist?", "Did Jesus Rise from the Dead?", and "Is Jesus God?" The lectures, reported and summarised in the *New Zealand Herald*, were published as *Three Crucial Questions about Jesus* (1994). Third, as part of the Open Lectures in the University of Otago, I spoke on "Plato and Paul on Immortality," a topic covered in my book *Raised Immortal* (1983).

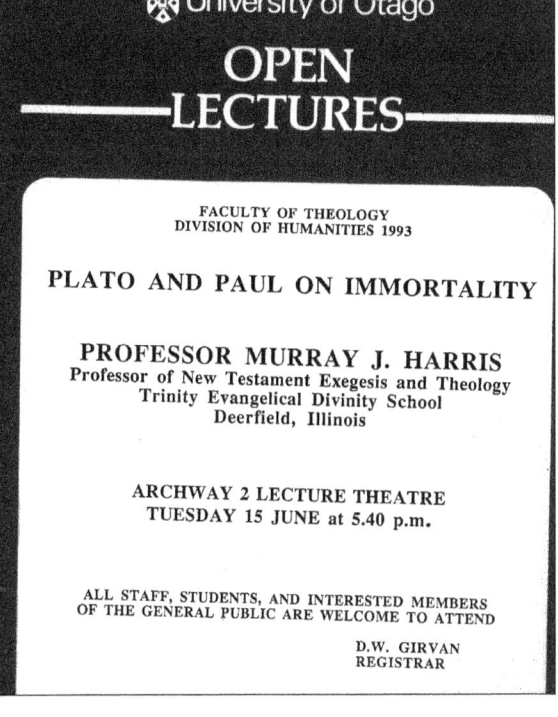

That Australasian tour included a visit to the Russell Museum in New Zealand's Bay of Islands. Russell was the first permanent European settlement in NZ. In this museum we were fascinated to discover these 1915 Rules for (Women) Teachers.

1. You will *not* marry during the term of your contract.
2. You are *not* to keep company with men.

3. You *must* be home between the hours of 8 p.m. and 6 a.m. unless attending a school function.
4. You may *not* loiter down town in ice-cream parlours.
5. You may *not* travel beyond the city limits without the permission of the Chairman of the Board.
6. You may *not* ride in a carriage or automobile with any man unless he is your Father or Brother.
7. You may *not* smoke cigarettes.
8. You may *not* dress in bright colours.
9. You may, *under no circumstances*, dye your hair.
10. You must wear *at least* two petticoats.
11. Your dresses must *not* be any shorter than two inches above the ankle.
12. To keep the school room neat and clean you must:
    - sweep the floor at least once daily
    - scrub the floor with hot soapy water at least once a week
    - clean the blackboards at least once a day
    - start the fire at 7 a.m. so that the room will be warm by 8 a.m.

(Reproduced, with knowledge of the Russell Museum, from the Museum copy of an unobtainable original)

Throughout my teaching career I have subscribed to *Time* and *Christianity Today*. I never imagined that my views about anything would be reported in these two magazines. The general contours of the "The Dr Norman L. Geisler Controversy" will be sketched below (chapter 12, pp. 90-92). Suffice it to note here that as a result of controversy over my view of the resurrection body of Christ, in 1991 *Christianity Today* published reviews of Dr Geisler's book, *The Battle for the Resurrection* and my response *From Grave to Glory: Resurrection in the New Testament* under the provocative title "Evangelical Fratricide." Then in 1995 *Time*'s cover story was "Can we still believe in miracles?" and included my defence of the reliability of the Gospels' testimony to the physical resurrection of Jesus. On the one hand, then, my view of the Resurrection was being inaccurately described and therefore unfairly criticized by fellow Evangelicals—Geisler and those influenced by him—and yet on the other hand it was being accurately portrayed and

Teaching Career (III)

indirectly endorsed in a secular magazine. To cap it off, the *Time* coverage of my view appeared between references to C. S. Lewis and Billy Graham! In these strange circumstances one writer discerned "God's magnanimous sense of humor."

1. (I Cor. 14:20) Τοῖς φρεσὶν τέλειοι γίνεσθε
   "Be mature in understanding"
2. (I Thess 5:21) Τὸ καλὸν κατέχετε
   "Hold fast/cling to what is good"
3. (Col. 4:5) Τὸν καιρὸν ἐξαγοραζόμενοι
   "Making/Make the most of every opportunity"
4. (Phil. 2:15) φαίνεσθε ὡς φωστῆρες ἐν κόσμῳ
   "You shine/Shine like stars in the universe"
5. (Phil. 3:13) Τοῖς ἔμπροσθεν ἐπεκτεινόμενος
   "Straining/Strain toward what is ahead"
6. (Col. 3:23) ὃ ἐὰν ποιῆτε ἐκ ψυχῆς ἐργάζεσθε
   "Work enthusiastically at whatever you do"
7. (1 Tim. 4:8) ἡ εὐσέβεια πρὸς πάντα ὠφέλιμός ἐστιν / Pietas ad omnia utilis est
   "The benefits of religion are limitless"
8. (1 Tim. 4:14) Μὴ ἀμέλει τοῦ ἐν σοὶ χαρίσματος
   "Do not neglect your spiritual endowment"
9. (1 Tim. 6:20) Τὴν παραθήκην φύλαξον
   "Guard what has been entrusted to you"
10. (Prov. 9:10) Principium sapientiae timor Domini
    "The fear of the Lord is the beginning of wisdom"

My requested suggestions for the motto of Trinity International University

During these final years at TEDS (now part of Trinity International University) I was surprised to receive two awards—the Faculty Member of the Year award in 1990, based on a student and faculty vote; and at our final chapel in June 1997 the announcement of the "Murray J. Harris Scholarship," funded by some of my recent students, as an "Annual award of $500 to be given to a full-time student who has combined ministry leadership with academic excellence during his or her study at Trinity." This was

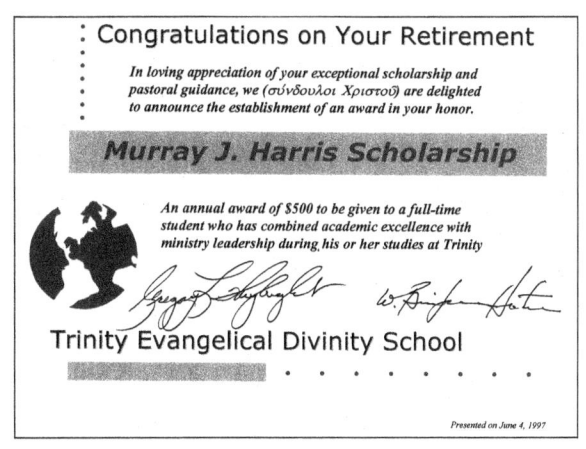

the first time a scholarship had been created and funded by students. In addition I was presented with a "memory scrapbook" compiled by students past and present "in honor of Dr Murray J. Harris and his 40 years of dedicated, Christ-centered ministry in scholarship and teaching throughout the world."

6

Teaching Career (IV)

THE BIBLE COLLEGE OF NEW ZEALAND (BCNZ) (1978–81)

OUR FIRST LETTER TO "Family and Friends" after our return "home" began this way. "We feel excused for resorting to the impersonality of a newsletter for two reasons: we have become Americanized, and we are missionaries on furlough in New Zealand after a prolonged term of service in a certain nameless emerging nation"!

My teaching at BCNZ covered the whole range of NT subjects: Greek, the exegesis of particular books, and broad topics such as the Kingdom of God or the NT view of the Church. Given the fact that most of the students were undergraduates and at this stage there were no masters programmes being offered, specialist subjects such as advanced Greek grammar or textual criticism were not taught. Most of the students were preparing for service in the local church, in para-church ministries, or abroad with mission agencies.

Jennifer had returned home in January 1970 to care for her mother, having been warned of the gravity of her mother's health. Now, eight years on and with a vast improvement in her health, we were able to welcome her into our home not as a guest but as a permanent resident, participating fully in our family life. There was action aplenty, for Oliver began school at Maungawhau Primary after his fifth birthday. He kept us theologically alert with his penetrating questions—as when he asked Jennifer, "When we go to heaven, will we see the holes in Jesus' hands? Will the nails still be in?" "No, I don't think the nails will be there, but we'll see where they were." "When I go to heaven, could I take two Bandaids for Jesus?" . . . "When Jesus came alive, why didn't he come through the rock? Why did he have his angels move it?"

On December 17, 1978, an article appeared in the *Sunday Times* entitled "The Rational Way of Giving" that justified the habit of generous giving at Christmas even among rationalists who denied the existence of Jesus. Further, the NZ Rationalist Association offered to give $500 to "anyone who could prove that the gospel Jesus was a historical person and that the gospels were accurate historical records." I was informed about the challenge and quickly penned a response that appeared in the Christmas eve edition of the *Times* on the other side of an enormous crossword, under the editorial title "Jesus existed, all right!" I stated I was not interested in the $500 but was concerned to establish the historicity of Jesus and the reliability of the Gospels. "Rationalists should hand over the $500" was the main heading of the next Challenge Weekly, reporting the "strong view" of Professor E. M. Blaiklock, Professor of Classics at the University of Auckland, that the claim is met and the case is proven and completely answered. Perhaps the greatest benefit that came from all the publicity was the subsequent Radio New Zealand broadcast reiterating the challenge and

Murray and Jennifer on the Empire State Building, New York

Teaching Career (IV)

the response, and the seven-page report of an interview with me in Reach Out.

The end of 1978 also saw the commencement of steps towards another possible adoption. Three overseas police clearances were obtained (Wildwood, Lake Forest, Highland Park) and four adoption classes attended. The letter of acceptance (Feb 23) of our candidacy stated that (i) usually only one out of three sets of approved parents receive a child; and (ii) there is usually a two-to-three year wait before adoption. On March 1, 1979 a baby girl was born, and at 3pm on March 20 Jessie Jane (as we called her) was collected from St Helen's Hospital. My 40th birthday was the previous day and Jennifer and I had agreed that we should not adopt a child after that! (Jane had been kept in hospital for over two weeks because of an eye infection). So once again we could trace God's gracious Fatherly hand on our circumstances.

The birth provoked two startlingly different literary responses—one from the faculty, the other from students. My learned Old Testament colleague, Bill Osborne, copying the abstruse style typical of papyrologists, chose to reflect on the announcement in the BCNZ paper.

> STOP PRESS!!! STOP PRESS!!!
> Congratulations to Dr. & Mrs Harris on the arrival of a little girl into their home, Jessie Jane (to be known as Jane).
>
> EXEGESIS OF A RECENTLY DISCOVERED INFANCY ORACLE
> Phenomenological analysis indicates the mythological form underlying the text.
>
> As is common in such materials the arrival of a child provides the stimulus for ontological reflections in the light of historical crises. This is indicated by the otherwise enigmatic superscription "stop press," twice repeated in the text. The expression relates the arrival of the child to the withdrawal of labour by printing unions known to have taken place early in the career of second-Harris in New Zealand (second-Harris is to be distinguished from first-Harris whose ministry is clearly located in North America).
>
> Editorial activity is evident in the explanatory note on the child's name. The full significance of the original name is clearly forgotten by the school of second-Harris' disciples known to have been located in the region of Henderson, and known as the "sons of Harris," hence the explanatory gloss. The mention of second-Harris' wife in the text indicates an awareness of her influence on his career, especially in periods of ontological crisis.

The significance of "Jessie Jane" is now lost to us, though various explanations have been attempted; none is fully satisfactory. It is perhaps best to assume corruption in the text, with the loss of the genitive of possession. Hence the text would appear to attempt to trace the Harris origins back to the Davidic dynasty of Jerusalem by reading "Jessie's Jane."

The student response (by Helen Wells and Carol Carr) was much more down-to-earth and was very clever.

My Favorite photos of Oliver and Jane as youngsters

You *had one child*, now you've two (2)(Three blind mice)
With two little children who look so sweet
The Harris family is complete,
They'll help their Daddy to exegete
And speak in Greek.

ELOCUTION CLASS
"The name of Jane is plainly on his brain."

RECITATION (with apologies to A. A. Milne)
Jane, Jane, the Harris's daughter,
(Not to be known as Jessie),

Teaching Career (IV)

> Takes great care of her father,
> Though she is only three (– weeks).
> Jane, Jane, the Harris's daughter,
> Said to her father, said she,
> "If you're going away to the college today,
> Then how about taking me?"
> Jane, Jane Harris's father
> Came to the college today,
> M. J. Harris, the father,
> Said he *had* to collect his pay.
> M. J. Harris, the father,
> Said to his daughter, said he,
> "The reason, young Jane, do I need to explain?
> —You're a very *dear* daughter to me!"

Shortly after settling into our new home and with the encouragement of some key people, I began a weekly study in our home for about ten young men of special potential. At their request they met for three hours "just to listen and to learn," as they put it. For two years we met each Wednesday evening, and of course I involved them in Socratic-type dialogue as we worked our way through the Gospel of Matthew and the book of Acts, discussing the text and the theological issues arising. Two of the men were natural humorists, so at regular intervals our home would vibrate with uncontrollable laughter. Deep friendships were formed, and appetites were whetted for more systematic Biblical and theological study. As a result, in 1980 I created Tyndale College, a part-time theological institution for University graduates who would remain in their profession but undertake study for the Melbourne College of Divinity BD degree (see further below, chapter 11, pp. 80-83). When I think of that group that soon blossomed to twenty in number and their present roles, I am reminded of the strategic importance of mentoring—a TV "anchor man," several businessmen, a high school principal, a judge, a surgeon, a BCNZ principal, and three University professors.

7

Teaching Career (V)

Tyndale House (TH) and the University of Cambridge (1981–86)

HISTORY AND INFLUENCE OF TYNDALE HOUSE (TH)

AT A KINGHAM HILL conference near Oxford in July 1941 an informal decision was reached by concerned evangelicals to create a residential centre and library for postgraduate Biblical research. In 1942 the first summer schools were held, at St Deiniol's Library in north Wales, and the first Tyndale Lectures delivered, in Oxford. The actual purchase of 36 Selwyn Gardens took place in December 1944, with the dedication of the building in January 1945. Then in 1955 a library building was attached to the House with thirteen study bedrooms on the first floor and twenty-one study desks in the library itself.

During my Wardenship a major extension to the library was undertaken (April 1984—May 1985), providing twelve extra study bays and a two-storeyed multipurpose hexagon that provided a seminar room and additional desk and shelving space on the first floor and space to display current periodicals and new books on the ground floor. In effect the space for readers was increased from twenty-five to over sixty. After prolonged hours spent with architects, builders and plumbers, I felt I had served an apprenticeship in each of these fields! So determined were we all to perfect our semi-circular study bays for two readers found throughout the library that we constructed a full-sized model and set it up in the garden so that readers could submit any recommendations for their improvement. This extension was opened debt-free, the cost of 250,000 pounds being met by over two hundred sources, mostly individuals.

TYNDALE HOUSE, CAMBRIDGE
Official Opening of the Library Extension
Saturday 11th May 1985
at 3 pm

Hugh Williamson Bill Kynes Brian Harris Dick France Donald Wiseman
Sir Kirby Laing Sir Norman Anderson Bishop John Taylor Murray Harris

It is hard to think of a setting more conducive to scholarly research than TH— with its library desks three paces away from the library stacks; with specialist, up-to-date holdings in all the major European languages that are immediately accessible, since books are on open shelving and may be used only in the library or the House, with no borrowing; with the library situated in a pleasant garden and quiet street ten minutes' walk from the University Library.

Well over one hundred doctorates in Biblical and related subjects, mostly from the University of Cambridge, have been gained by students based at TH. One scholar, Dr D. A. Carson, himself a Cambridge PhD who has spent several sabbaticals at TH, has observed that TH wields an influence among evangelical Biblical scholars worldwide that is vastly disproportionate to its size. In a nutshell, TH is a study center designed to produce Bible experts who are committed to serving both local churches and the global Church.

TH is closely associated with the Universities and Colleges Christian Fellowship (UCCF, formerly the InterVarsity Fellowship [IVF]), its parent body, so that TH personnel are UCCF employees. In a similar way, TH and the Tyndale Fellowship (TF) are intimately related: TF study groups are held at TH; TF appointments are confirmed by the TH Council; TF monies are handled by and through TH; the Warden is an *ex officio* member of the TF Committee; and the *Tyndale Bulletin* is the organ of both the TF and TH.

So then, TH is known throughout the world as a leading centre of informed conservative scholarship in the service of the worldwide Church, while the TF is widely recognized as a body of scholars who have decisively shown that true evangelicalism is not synonymous with obscurantism or second-rate scholarship.

For further detail on these matters, see T. A. Noble, *Tyndale House and Fellowship: The First Sixty Years* (Leicester: Inter-Varsity, 2006).

APPOINTMENT TO THE WARDENSHIP OF TH

My appointment to this post was a protracted process. In mid-February 1981 I received a UCCF letter indicating the vacancy of the Wardenship and soliciting expressions of interest. But by now we felt settled "at home" in New Zealand, so I disregarded the issue, also remembering the succession of distinguished previous Wardens—Sir Norman Anderson, Dr Leon Morris, Rev Derek Kidner, and Dr Richard France. But then a letter came from Alan Millard, a previous librarian at TH and later Rankin Professor of Hebrew and Ancient Semitic Languages at the University of Liverpool. Alan knew of me from our two-month stay in Cambridge in 1976 when we attended the same church, and from his friendship with Professor Bruce. The letter gently suggested we give the opportunity serious consideration—which we did, so that we received more information and submitted our resumé and proposed referees. From the previous Warden we received a sixty-minute tape giving answers to some forty-nine questions we had posed! A week-long visit was arranged for July. Our return on a Continental Airways flight from Los Angeles was memorable because by an error we travelled first class, which was most appropriate since we were teaching a class at BCNZ in Henderson at 8:45am after landing at 7:15.

The first response from the TH Council was ambiguous. "We are unable to make a decision at this time," which we took to be a negative decision, but a flurry of confidential communication made it clear that two issues had prevented a firm decision at the time of my visit. First, there was some uncertainty about the roles and therefore the qualifications of the Warden; they were looking for a non-existent Dr Gabriel, one source observed. Second, during my visit three key members of the academic sub-committee were absent because of the summer academic break—Donald Wiseman, Alan Millard, and Howard Marshall. On August 24 I received a formal invitation to assume the Wardenship, an invitation that was "warm and unanimous." In two regards the Council was breaking with tradition regarding Wardens—apparently it was not an insuperable problem that I was not a graduate of Oxford or Cambridge (= "Oxbridge") and not an Anglican.

TEACHING AND RELATIONSHIP WITH THE UNIVERSITY

To complete my delight in accepting my new role as Warden, an invitation came from the Secretary of the Faculty Board of Divinity of the University to become a member of the Faculty. Accordingly, each year I attended the faculty meetings in the famous Lightfoot Room. This was also the venue for the weekly New Testament seminar when papers were read by visiting scholars or local researchers. I was privileged to give a paper on "The Logos Christology of the Fourth Gospel in light of Professor James Dunn's *Christology in the Making*."

What is distinctive about an Oxbridge education is the central place given to the one-on-one seminar between teacher and student that complements the University lecture. So it was that I sometimes served as a supervisor for students studying NT subjects such as the Synoptic Gospels or Theology and Ethics. But apart from that formal teaching, there was the opportunity not only to encourage and direct individual readers in their research but also to initiate informal fortnightly TH seminars relevant to the readers. When I arrived at TH there were several doctoral researchers whose writing had stalled, so my first seminar was entitled "How to bring your thesis to a successful conclusion" that was partially summed up in my oft-quoted dictum, "The first requirement is the progressive surrender of ideals of perfection." It is natural for someone undertaking doctoral research to imagine that they must master every issue that impinges on their central thesis. Another topic of perpetual relevance was "How to conduct yourself in an oral defence of your thesis." You can imagine my pleasure when an examinee reported that the first response of his examiners was to congratulate him on how well he had handled himself in the oral!

RESPONSIBILITIES OF THE WARDEN

Although the primary responsibility of the Warden is his own research and writing, I found that during the first year, administrative issues such as the booking of accommodation and desks and the maintenance of the property took a major part of my time. In fact, my first task on arrival was repairing the cistern in the men's toilet! But relief came in the second year with the appointment of a part-time bursar, a role that became full-time thereafter. In allocating the single rooms above the library for any year, priority was given to library readers but there were always students following courses of study or research in other fields such as education, engineering, chemistry, or computer science. These students contributed towards maintaining the sanity of the theological researchers!

The welfare of the residents and readers was a paramount concern. On Monday evenings the residents and families from the three flats in the House met for an *agape* meal—without the Lord's Supper or the "holy kiss." Fellowship in eating led naturally to fellowship in worship and intercession. For the library readers I instituted a weekly chapel service as the focal point for our corporate life. Never before had I been able in any corporate setting to read the Scripture for the day in Greek—but here it was totally appropriate as we worked our way through Hebrews week by week in exposition.

These two features—the fortnightly seminars (see p. 50) and the weekly chapels—served to remind us all that the pursuit of excellence in Biblical research and writing is a spiritual task and calling, not a purely academic exercise. There is no substitute for the maintenance of right relations with God. As the foundation stone of the Library expresses it "The fear of the Lord is the beginning of wisdom" (Proverbs 1:7)," or as it might be rendered "The first principle of knowledge is to hold the Lord in awe."

To fulfill the task of publicizing the work of TH I twice visited the USA. This was appropriate since (1) over the five previous years sixty percent of our regular library users had been from North America but only six percent of our donation income had been from that source; (2) the Library Extension Appeal Fund was within 35,000 pounds of its target of 250,000 pounds; and (3) North American gifts were tax-deductible (since donations were channelled through IVCF in Madison or Toronto). My 1984 itinerary, Los Angeles—Kansas City—Miami—Chicago—Grand Rapids—Toronto, proved too strenuous (an itinerary that I myself had created!) and I ended up in hospital in St Louis. But either by personal visit or by taped conversation I was able to contact the key persons in each of these areas. Response everywhere was warm and positive. I spoke to church leaders who were responsible for the allocation of missionary giving, to wealthy businessmen, and to former readers of the library, leaving them with publicity material. Interestingly, it later turned out that for some years there had been serious discussion among members of the Institute for Biblical Research (the North American equivalent of the TF) about the possible creation of a TH-like library in some University city in the USA. But it became clear to them that they could never reproduce TH and so the vision was abandoned.

As a result of the two visits (1984 and 1985 after a meeting of the NIV Committee) and the enthusiastic and creative energy of Dr Paul E. Leonard, three regional TH support groups in the USA and one in Canada were established, each comprising an honorary deputation secretary and a group of seven to ten persons including senior scholars and representatives of the churches. Recent TH publicity cites the opinion of Dr Duane Litfin, a former President of Wheaton College, Illinois: "The American Christian community in particular has benefited immeasurably from the work of Tyndale House and holds a major stake in helping to keep it strong."

HIGHLIGHTS FROM OUR TH YEARS

My first invitation to speak at a College chapel came from Peterhouse, the oldest of the Cambridge Colleges. Seated at High Table next to the Master for the meal that followed, I was told, "Dr Harris, look around at this Dining Hall. There have been three meals served here every day for the last seven hundred and fifty years!" The effect was stunning for someone whose oldest home university (Otago) was not yet one hundred and twenty years old. Other chapel engagements included St John's and Trinity Hall. How could one forget the quiet and revealing conversations at the socials of the Faculty of the Divinity School with renowned scholars such as Dr John Robinson (of *Honest To God* fame), or Dr Ernst Bammel, or Professor Henry Chadwick?

The Cambridge Inter-Collegiate Christian Union (CICCU) was formed in 1877 (and the parallel OICCU at Oxford in 1879) and is best known for the "Cambridge Seven," students who in 1885 decided to become missionaries to China with the China Inland Mission. I had the opportunity to teach the Bible Study Group Leaders over eight sessions on the book of Romans, and a series on the Introduction to all the NT books (authorship, date, purpose etc.).

Opportunities arose for participation in some television and radio programmes—the London Weekend Television 1986 *Credo* programme on "The Christian View of Life After Death;" a 1984 BBC radio 4 programme "Poles Apart," along with six other participants, recorded in Auckland (!) Castle in Durham, a debate involving the Bishop of Durham and his controversial views (see below, chapter 10, pp. 67-68); a Cambridge radio programme regarding an Anglican Synod paper, with Dr Rowan Williams, later the Archbishop of Canterbury. Conferences or lectures abroad included the Irish UCCF Associates' annual conference at Greystones in Co. Wicklow, on "Men and Women in Christ;" and at the Freie Theologische Akademie in Giessen (then in West Germany) a series on "Jesus as *Theos*."

Of special significance at TH itself, one must mention two items. (1) The completion of the six-volume *Gospel Perspectives* series, published by the JSOT Press in Sheffield and Eisenbraun's in the USA, which forms a robust, informed defence of the historical reliability of the four Gospels by thirty-three NT scholars from seven nationalities. Dr Craig L. Blomberg's popularisation of the major findings of the whole series (*The Historical Reliability of the Gospels* [Downers Grove: IVP, 2007, second edition]) was a suitable climax for the protracted effort of many people over seven years. (2) The official opening of the library extension in May 1985 (see above, chapter 7, p. 48). I will never forget several related events. Our main speaker for the day, Professor F. F. Bruce, did not arrive, owing to a breakdown of his train from Buxton "in the middle of nowhere." That was not the era of cell phones! Our chairman of the day, Professor Donald Wiseman, admirably rose to the occasion. Then on a brilliant summer's day, the impulse to break into and inspect the new premises proved irresistible to one intruder. There was a resounding crash of broken glass and then there appeared a perfectly round hole in a window—as a pigeon, which had apparently been perched in the garden's giant ilex tree, viewing the even larger ilex in the window, shot into *and out of* Room 13 above the library, leaving only a dozen white feathers and a spray of glass slivers as its visiting card! Another memorable event involved the first Warden, Sir Norman Anderson. I well remember his exuberance when he saw the library's new form. "Murray, this is *great!*"

Teaching Career (V)

Then off he went immediately, and in fifteen minutes reappeared with Lady Anderson, showing her over the premises as excitedly as if they had just returned to their new home after their honeymoon!

My administrative responsibilities inevitably brought me into close contact with two remarkable men. The chairman of the TH Council was Professor Donald Wiseman who served in this capacity for 30 years. During the Second World War he was PA to Air Vice-Marshal Keith Park, who was in charge of the Fighter Group responsible for the defence of SE Britain during the Battle of Britain. He was awarded the USA Bronze Star Medal for his services as Chief Intelligence Officer of the Mediterranean Allied Tactical Air Force during 1943–44. As an academic he was Professor of Assyriology in the University of London for twenty years. We served together on the NIV Committee on Bible Translation and its British subcommittee. The chairman of the Business Committee of the TH Council was Sir Kirby Laing, a fifth-generation member of the Laing family's British construction industry. He had served as chairman or president of numerous construction associations or councils. One would often see towering above all buildings the massive sign "LAING." His confirmatory signature was required on my secretarial minutes of our meetings before they became official and were distributed!

We counted Robert Gordon and Hugh Williamson among our friends. Little did we realize that in time each would become a Regius Professor of Hebrew, Gordon at Cambridge and Williamson at Oxford.

FAMILY DURING OUR TH YEARS

Family holidays in Wales were always a highlight of the year. We used to stay in my brother Don's cottage on a farm in Snowdonia, North Wales. Visits to castles were always a favorite for the children, whether Harlech Castle near Porthmadog or Penrhyn Castle near Bangor.

Apart from her demanding task of keeping the family fed, clothed and happy, and doing Tyndale entertaining, Jennifer helped to keep the TH garden in order, made quilted garments for sale to local buyers, and acted as secretary of "Women Together," an interdenominational Christian outreach group in Cambridge that met four times a year. Their aim was to arrange for well-known celebrities to speak of their faith and to present the Good News in pleasant, relaxed surroundings such as the local Arts Theatre or the Graduate Centre. Speakers included Patricia St John, author of the children's books *The Tanglewoods' Secret* and *Treasures in the Snow*, and Lady Elizabeth Catherwood, wife of Sir Fred, the local European MP. The venture proved highly successful, with tickets sold out weeks in advance and numbers making professions of faith.

Bicycles were (and are) the order of the day in Cambridge, so that our family of four used to cycle together to church. During the second half of the service, Jennifer and I would take turns to walk around neighbouring streets with the children. Oliver will never forget the time when, providentially, we came across a man who was about to throw a boy's trolley into a large skip. We saved him the trouble and later remodelled what became Oliver's pride and joy and constant companion. He never tired of taking our Sheltie called Lady for walks across the spacious fields near the River Cam. On one such occasion he spotted a bicycle submerged in the murky waters of one of the Cam's small tributaries. We rescued it, washed and drained it clean, and took it to the local police station cycle store. We were told that if the owner was not found in three months, the bicycle would be Oliver's. Never did the days pass so slowly for Oliver, but his patience and good fortune—or providential provision—made him the possessor of a brand new racing bicycle worth 160 pounds to replace his rather dilapidated bike. Perhaps someone, needing a quick ride somewhere, had picked up the nearest bicycle, used it, and then discarded it in the river!

Jane's claim to fame during those days arose from the fact that she was in the same class at Newnham Croft Primary School as the only daughter of Professor Stephen Hawking of immortal fame. In fact, she and I attended Lucy's birthday party in the Hawking home. We would often see Hawking at school functions shooting across the grass in his motorized and adapted wheelchair. He was a hard man to catch, whether in space or on the earth! At a later time, after our third USA interlude and return to New Zealand, Jane was treated with awe because she had *actually* and *regularly* seen Scotty Pippin, the Chicago Bulls NBA star, when she was serving in a local candy shop. Her friend had a full-sized picture of Pippin on her New Zealand bedroom wall!

Regularly on Saturday afternoons Jennifer would drive the children and me three miles north to Grantchester Village where we would inflate our two rubber boats and quietly float or paddle down the River Cam back to Cambridge. The river banks were quite high with no visible signs of human life so we felt we were in a world apart. After Jennifer met us two hours later, I would cycle off to a free organ recital at King's College Chapel. What a blissful Saturday!

8

Teaching Career (VI)

VISITING LECTURESHIPS

OVER THE YEARS I have been privileged to give lectureships of shorter or longer periods in various institutions. I have not included here lectures given at Trinity extension courses across the USA.

1967 Winona Lake School of Theology in Winona Lake, Indiana ("Criticism of the Gospels"; "Early Christian Doctrine")

1970 Tyndale Lecture in Cambridge, England ("2 Corinthians 5:1-10: Watershed in Paul's Eschatology?")

1973 25th Anniversary of the Evangelical Theological Society in Wheaton, Illinois ("Paul's view of Death in 2 Corinthians 5:1-10")

1975 InterVarsity Silver Lake Camp near Minneapolis, Minnesota ("Issues in 1 Corinthians")

1976 John Wesley College in East Lansing, Michigan ("Life and Letters of Paul")

1977 North Park College and Theological Seminary in Chicago, Illinois ("Petrine Epistles")

1978 Midwestern Section of the Evangelical Theological Society in Wheaton, Illinois ("Jesus as God")

1980 TSCF Conference in Auckland, New Zealand ("Called to Advance: Studies in 2 Corinthians")

1981 Auckland Graduate Christian Fellowship in Auckland ("Strategy for Christian Warfare in the 1980s and 1990s")

1984 InterVarsity Irish Associates Conference in Greystones, Co. Wicklow ("Men and Women in Christ")

1986 Free Theological Academy in Giessen, (West) Germany ("Jesus as *Theos*")

1988 Woodlands Conference Centre in Christchurch, New Zealand ("Studies in 1 and 2 Corinthians;" "Colossians: Christ and his Church")

1989 Southern Baptist Theological Seminary in Louisville, Kentucky ("Exegesis of 1 and 2 Corinthians")

1990 Faith Evangelical Chapel in Acton, Massachusetts ("The Stewardship of Life")

1990 West Point Grey Baptist Church in Vancouver ("Studies in 2 Corinthians")

1990 Regent College in Vancouver ("Plato and Paul on Immortality")

1992 Evangelical Theological Society's 44th Annual Meeting in San Francisco ("Jesus as *Theos*")

1993 InterVarsity of Lake Forest College in Lake Forest, Illinois ("Resurrection of Jesus")

1993 Bible College of New Zealand at University of Auckland in Auckland ("Three Crucial Questions about Jesus")

1993 University of Otago Open Lectures in Dunedin, New Zealand ("Plato and Paul on Immortality")

1993 Society for the Study of Early Christianity at Macquarie University in Sydney, Australia ("The Use of *Theos* as a Christological Title in the New Testament")

1997 Moore Theological College in Sydney ("Slave of Christ")

1998 Pathways College in Auckland ("The Christian Sacraments")

1998 Teapot Valley Christian Camp near Nelson, New Zealand ("2 Corinthians")

1998–2002, 2004 Winter Bible School at Totara Springs, Matamata, Waikato ("2 Corinthians, Colossians, Important Themes in Paul's Letters, Hebrews, Relating Paul's Letters to the Book of Acts, John 1—12")

1999 Woodend Christian Camp near Christchurch ("Colossians")

1999 China Evangelical Seminary, Hong Kong ("The Agenda for Biblical Studies in the 21st Century. Issues and Challenges;" "The Agenda for the Biblical Student and Scholar in the 21st Century. Issues and Challenges")

1999 Evangel College, Hong Kong ("Why March 25th is more important than December 25th;" "Christian Stewardship")

Teaching Career (VI)

2003 Mount Aspiring College Evening class, Wanaka, New Zealand ("The Life, Times, and Teaching of Jesus of Nazareth;" "The Life and Teaching of the Apostle Paul")

2003 Cambridge High School Evening Class ("The Life, Times, and Teaching of Jesus of Nazareth")

2016—2017 Cambridge Baptist Church in Cambridge, New Zealand ("The Life, Times, and Teaching of Jesus of Nazareth;" "The Life and Teaching of the Apostle Paul")

When the reader surveys all these speaking engagements in so many different settings and places, curiosity might prompt you to ask, "As you reflect on all these occasions, what was the most humorous episode and what was the most embarrassing?" The answers are clear.

In the Sunday morning service of a large Vancouver church, after one of my addresses in the annual January Bible Study Series, I was warmly thanked by the minister. Then followed a long pause, which had the effect of riveting the congregation's attention on the pastor. He proceeded to announce his resignation! A corporate gasp went up across the large sanctuary. I wondered, "Whatever did I say in my talk that could possibly have precipitated this immediate and dramatic response?" After the service the pastor apologised to me profusely, and in a follow-up letter hinted at serious tensions within the church and said that he had debated long and hard whether he should go ahead with the announcement but felt that events were moving rather quickly so that he needed to do what he did, when he did. He assured me that this interruption to the series would not remove its benefit.

The most humorous episode occurred in Hong Kong when I was addressing the student body and staff at Evangel College on the topic of Christian stewardship. Of course, as was appropriate for the occasion, I was dressed in a suit and tie. In the course of encouraging simplicity of life, I appealed to the life of Albert Schweitzer as a splendid example of living simply. When a reporter noticed that Schweitzer had travelled in a second class carriage in a British train, he asked him, "Dr Schweitzer, why were you not travelling first class?" He replied, "Because there was no third class." Then I mentioned another reporter's question. "Dr Schweitzer, why do you always wear the same white jacket and the same tie? Why not buy another tie?" "What? For only one neck?" The point clearly registered with the students. When I had finished my lecture, one of the students expressed their gratitude for my visit and then surprised everyone by presenting me with a gift from the College that I was encouraged to open. There, in a specially constructed box, was one of the College's exquisite and distinctive ties. Everyone exploded in uncontrollable laughter!

Again and again over the years students have expressed appreciation for the prayers I offer at the beginning of class. Rarely do I offer public prayers *ex tempore*. They are not written out but are carefully prepared, because the teacher has the awesome responsibility of leading the whole class with their variety of needs before the throne of grace. Any passage of Scripture about to be discussed affords truth that can readily and appropriately be converted into prayer, if we recall the essential ingredients of prayer—adoration, confession, thanksgiving, supplication (ACTS).

9

Adjusting to life in the USA

"Kiwis in the Land of the Eagle"

IMMIGRATION ISSUES

IN AUGUST 1967, CARRYING the necessary papers from Trinity, we took the train from Manchester across to the US Embassy in Liverpool. Since there was some uncertainty about our immigration status, we were issued with a B1/2 visa (B1 for tourism, B2 for business) and the following was written in my passport: "Facilitate admission pending clarification of status by I&NS Chicago."

This need for "clarification (or adjustment) of status" seems to have characterised much of our subsequent relationship with the Immigration and Naturalisation Service in the USA. How temporary or permanent was the residence of four Kiwis in the Land of the Eagle? (The kiwi, a flightless bird, is one of New Zealand's national symbols, so New Zealanders are often called Kiwis). Over the years we often needed to visit the immigration offices in downtown Chicago, where the crowds of hopefuls were sorted out in a preliminary fashion on the ground floor (= first floor in American parlance) and then sent to the appropriate endless queues on the first (= second) floor of the massive building. Our initial visa was subsequently changed to H2, a temporary worker visa with an approved US employer that could be renewed each year, and then to a H1 visa for a "distinguished alien in the arts or sciences." As it happened, we had greater problems with little Oliver's visas, as a three-year old. After a second extension of his visitor's visa, he was automatically placed on a "deportation list"! After a third extension, he was "paroled," to enable him to visit New Zealand with Jennifer.

On our return to the USA in 1986 we began the lengthy process of applying for resident alien status. First, we had to apply to the Illinois Department of Employment Security for a work permit, to ensure there was no qualified and willing US citizen who could fill my projected permanent post. When the position was advertised nationally in the *Chronicle for Higher Education*, a man who had a doctorate from Bob Jones University and was currently working on a farm applied and Trinity was obliged to interview him! The second advertisement in the *Chronicle* was made so specific to my qualifications and experience that no one else on earth could possibly have met the description of the post. In the end we all received the "green card" (which actually is blue) as resident aliens, so my position at Trinity was potentially permanent.

LANGUAGE DIFFERENCES

Language is fascinating. As one learns a foreign language, the final challenge is to master the distinctive idioms of the new language. As when a German librarian joined the staff of the Cambridge University Library and reassured the readers, "I am totally at your disposal. You may dispose of me in any way you vish."

But in moving from British or New Zealand English to American English it is less the idioms than word associations or changes in word usage that are the challenge for new arrivals. So it was for me. As I, a newcomer to the US, was settling into my new office in a reassigned apartment block, I approached two young secretaries for help and blithely asked, "Do you happen the have a rubber for me to use?" I had not learned that in the US a "rubber" was a condom, not an eraser as it had always been for me! Or again, when my wife and I were first entertaining my advisees with their wives and infant children in our home, I sought to help a mother who was obviously struggling with holding a cup and saucer as well as a child. "Here," I said, "Let me nurse your daughter for a while." I had not learned that in the US "nurse" meant "breast feed," not "gently hold"!

One characteristic of American English, perhaps reflecting the generous disposition of Americans in general, is the tendency to bolster the language by using adverbs with superlatives. This being so, Americans, more often than reticent Britishers, will speak of something as "the very best" or as "very unique." I sometimes have illustrated this tendency to water down the original meanings of words by adding auxiliaries by reminding students of President Gerald Ford's memorable first words aboard Air Force One after the resignation of President Richard Nixon. "This must be the most saddest day in American history." Or take the word "professor," that in Britain and the Commonwealth refers to the highest rank of the teacher, so that if a person holds both a doctorate and is a professor, the latter description is regularly used. But in the US the term "professor" has become somewhat debased, so the sequence in a tertiary institution is "assistant professor," associate professor, full (!) professor, and if a doctorate is held, that is the preferred term of address.

AMERICAN CUSTOMS

I believe some distinctive American customs are to be commended and should be imitated by other countries. One is the traditionally early start to the working day. Our son's school bus used to pick him up at 7:15am. At Woodlands Conference Centre in the Adirondacks the seminars I taught began at 6:35am.

Some customs were surprising. There was a delightful willingness to continue family traditions in public. During our first restaurant meal in the US, the waitress twice came to our table and left while our host engaged in a lengthy, round-the-world prayer. Another custom proved to be both acutely embarrassing and, after the event, quite hilarious. I was totally unaware of the custom that a formal funeral procession, however long, had right-of-way at traffic lights. A close colleague and friend of mine at Trinity, Dr Tom McComiskey, had suddenly died. I had participated at his funeral and was driving the middle car of about forty vehicles, each with the customary beacon on the roof, that made up the procession for the drive to the cemetery for the final committal. When we reached a major intersection and the lights turned red in front of me, of course I stopped, along with the twenty cars behind me. Traffic flowed across our path for what seemed to me like an eternity. Fortunately, someone behind me in the procession knew the way to the cemetery, so we arrived just in time for the actual interment.

AMERICAN HUMOR

As I have experienced American humor among my students and elsewhere, I would describe it as ready and enthusiastic, yet sometimes muted and sophisticated in the British style. At my first routine visit to an American doctor, I was asked the standard questions. "Do you smoke?" "No." "Do you drink?" "No." "Do you drink tea?" "No." "Do you drink coffee?" "No." The doctor looked at me over his glasses. "My, Mr Harris. You are a paragon of virtue!"

For American high school students, the standard set of guides to literary classics is *Cliffs Notes. Your key to the classics*. I was once presented with a new guide that had the same cover format and color. *Cliffs Notes . . . on Harris's Colossians and Philemon . . . Exegetical Guide to the Greek New Testament*. When we left Trinity in 1978 I was given a new specially printed edition of the *Chicago Tribune* with the heading emblazoned in large black type. *MURRAY HARRIS LEAVES 611B IN TEARS*. Then when we were about to leave Trinity in 1997, at a mock ceremony at the conclusion of my class on Pauline Theology an inscribed plaque was presented to me.

> *In recognition of his sage learning and erudition*
>
> > *this document is presented to*
> > DR MURRAY J. HARRIS
>
> DIPLOMA of ANCIENT KIWI WISDOM
>
> *Awarded this fifth day of June in the nineteen*
> *hundred and ninety seventh year of our Lord by*
> *the graduating seniors and other students of the*
> *Pauline Theology class of the same year,*
> *whose signatures are displayed below*

At the time of New Zealand's triumph in the America's cup in 1995, I was given a page from *The New York Times International* entitled "The Little Nation That Could." "While New Zealand calls itself a 'nation of sailors,' the country is not without its heroes and champions in other sports and academic scholarship." There is a list, with some pictures, of New Zealand world champions in track and field, marathon, cross-country, rugby, golf, and auto racing—and New Testament Studies, Murray J. Harris, Professor of New Testament at Trinity Evangelical Divinity School.

10

Writing Ventures

GENERAL OBSERVATIONS

FOR THE TASK OF writing as well as speaking it is imperative to have a sophisticated filing system, enabling anything read from any source that may prove useful to be filed away, be it the original or a photocopy of a page or article. My nine hundred or so files ran from Abba to Zionism and were housed in seven four-drawer metal filing cabinets. (I know that in these high-tech days there are other ways of storing material, but can anything replace the shuffling of papers on a desk?). My list of topics began as an abridgement and then expansion of a list for pastors published by Baker Book House. My advice has always been that one's system is adequate if any item needed can be found in less than thirty seconds.

All too often evangelical scholars have had their writing projects dictated by editorial invitation. A publishing house decides that the time has come for a new commentary series or a multi-volume new dictionary designed for a particular audience. An editor is appointed and invitations go out to evangelical Biblical scholars throughout the world, soliciting their participation and holding out the irresistible carrot of an advance on royalties. I have known not a few evangelical scholars who in their writing ministry simply bounce—or lurch—from one deadline to another. Some of my earlier writing involved book reviews, general articles, and dictionary articles. But in recent years my focus has particularly been on identifying specific needs within the field of NT studies, and seeking to "plug" some of those gaps. Examples of my efforts to meet particular needs include the following.

When some scholars were driving a wedge between resurrection and immortality, I sought to defend both concepts as being genuinely Pauline in *Raised Immortal* (1983). While there have always been many commentaries on the Greek text of New Testament books, there was a need for commentaries that give all the necessary help with the details and nuances of the Greek but also seek to bridge the gap between study and pulpit by providing expanded paraphrases of the text and homiletical suggestions (thus *Colossians and Philemon*, 1991, and the ongoing *Exegetical Guides to the Greek New Testament*). Given the surprising fact that a detailed treatment of the use of *theos* as a title of Christ had never been written in any language throughout church history, I produced a three-hundred-and-eighty-page work on the topic (*Jesus as God*, 1992). Because the majority of English translations avoided the use of the term "slave" to depict the relation of the believer to the Lord Christ, I endeavoured to show the legitimacy of the term in that context in *Slave of Christ: A New Testament Metaphor for Total Devotion to Christ* (1999). Since there had been no book-length treatment of prepositions in the Greek New Testament since 1919, this gap was met by *Prepositions and Theology in the Greek New Testament* (2012). Although there was no shortage of booklets on John 3:16, a need remained for a close grammatical investigation of the verse—hence *John 3:16: What's It All About?* (2015).

APOLOGETIC WRITING

In general terms the apologist seeks to defend the accuracy and trustworthiness of the Biblical text, or the orthodox understanding of the Bible, often against the backdrop of widely publicised alternative views.

Reference has already been made (in chapter 6) to my 1978 defence of the existence of Jesus against the Rationalist denial that he ever existed. More detailed treatments of this issue followed in a chapter entitled "References to Jesus in early classical authors" in Volume 5 of *Gospel Perspectives* (1985) and in the first chapter ("Did Jesus Exist?") of my *Three Crucial Questions* (1994). I have also already mentioned (in chapter 5) the 1995 *Time* article on miracles in which I contribute to the defence of one of the greatest miracles of all—the resurrection of Jesus.

In December 1998 the *NZ Herald* published an article by Dr James Veitch, a professor of religious studies at Victoria University in Wellington, New Zealand, that alleged that the Christmas story as recorded in the Gospels is simply a gripping fairy tale, a mesmerising myth with magic all of its own. He also proposed that Christ's wisdom, buried for centuries in the pageantry of the Bethlehem fairy tale, needed to be rescued from "Santa." My published rejoinder, appearing under the editorial heading "Gospels' record of Christmas events historically correct," focused on Luke's demonstrable reliability as an ancient historian. I pointed out that "the heart of the Christian faith is not the Sermon on the Mount but the Cross on the Hill, not Jesus as a teacher of wisdom who simply gives us good advice but Jesus as the Saviour of humankind who himself provides us with a way to be reconciled to God." The article concludes with the words "But there is a real sense in which Jesus does not need to be "rescued" by anyone or from anything. He is well able to care for himself, as he has been for 2000 years. Sceptics come and go but he goes on for ever. At present they grapple with his living Spirit but they do not face him in person—yet."

No one will doubt that my most significant foray into apologetics involved the writings of Dr David E. Jenkins, formerly Professor of Theology at Leeds University, and appointed Bishop of Durham in July 1984. He had scandalised multitudes of people both inside and outside the church during previous months by his impromptu and designedly provocative comments, often made into a journalist's microphone or before a TV camera, that seemed to call into question two cardinal doctrines of the Christian faith— the Virgin Birth and especially the Resurrection of Jesus. Some months later, after I had participated in a BBC radio programme with the Bishop and others, I became convinced that his views were being unfairly represented in the press but also that his views did not conform to the testimony of the New Testament. Thus was born a thirty-two page booklet, *Easter in Durham* (= the view of the Resurrection in the writings of the Bishop of Durham) that summarises the Bishop's views in detail, quoting extensively from his own writings, and that undertakes an appraisal of his views in the light of New Testament teaching. The Bishop of London, Dr Graham Leonard (second in seniority in the Church of England: Canterbury—London—Durham!) kindly contributed the Preface. Courtesy of a substantial gift from a friend of Tyndale House, one thousand three hundred copies of the booklet were sent (with Dr Leonard's encouragement) to all Church of England bishops and suffragan bishops, archdeacons, and city and rural deans. This is probably the most widely read document I have ever written; it was reviewed (favorably!) in numerous papers and periodicals (from the *Guardian* to the *Harvester*) in several countries. Here was a student of Scripture quietly seeking "to contend for the faith that was once for all entrusted to the saints" (Jude 3). (More details about the controversy may be found in chapter eighteen of *From Grave to Glory*).

My first live TV experience was in August 1998 on the Holmes programme, a national current affairs programme on NZ's TV 1. Dr Robert Funk, the prime mover behind the Jesus Seminar and their subsequent book *The Five Gospels*, was touring New Zealand, seeking to popularize the findings of the Seminar. We only had a twelve-minute slot, but (now Sir) Paul Holmes's nightly show—immediately after the evening news—was the most widely watched programme of its kind. Against Funk's assertion about the historical unreliability of the Gospels, I pointed to Luke's claim that he had carefully researched the earliest eyewitness sources—personal and literary—that were relevant to his transcript of the life and teaching of Jesus (Luke 1:1–4). Modern historians rightly take seriously any such claim by ancient historians and treat them as innocent of error until proved guilty rather than guilty until proved innocent. At the points where we can check Luke's accuracy against contemporary evidence, he emerges as totally innocent. Many expressed appreciation to me for representing "informed conservatism" so winsomely. I think Professor Funk may have been a little surprised to learn that there were reputable NT scholars even in New Zealand, especially since I told him that in another context I had consulted his doctoral dissertation on Paul's use of the Greek definite article.

"Wife's death video" was the front page heading in the NZ Herald of September 14, 2012. Suffering from multiple sclerosis (MS), Rosie Mott had prepared a video in which she declared she was not committing suicide but rather was euthanising herself. Her husband had prepared a death kit but was not present when she died, and in spite of pleading guilty of assisting in the suicide he was discharged without conviction, partly because the judge considered his culpability to be low. Since Jennifer had suffered from MS for many years, I immediately prepared a thousand-word response, describing an alternative way of reacting to the ravages of MS and summarising the arguments against voluntary euthanasia or doctor-assisted suicide. "We both want to continue to enjoy our mutual love and friendship as long as we can . . . We believe life is a unique and priceless God-given gift. It should therefore always be greatly treasured and carefully preserved . . . Killing with kindness is not an option for us. Living with gratitude is our choice." Although the article was promptly submitted to the *Herald* for their consideration, it was not published there. (Editors are perhaps more interested in the sensational and startling than the mundane). It found a home in a Christian magazine, *The Challenge*.

From my efforts as an apologist I have learned several important things in this area.

- You often must act quickly, grasping an opportunity as soon as it arises. That is, one must use "the psychological moment" (see Col 3:5), even though it involves the temporary suspension of a current project.

- One apologetic encounter almost invariably leads to additional opportunities to speak or write, opportunities for oneself and for others.

- You must carefully examine and master the views of your "opponents," so that there can never be the charge that you have demolished a "straw man."

- Whenever possible, solicit your colleagues' evaluation of any written piece before it is published, and of any oral communication after it is given.

- The act of "fronting up" publicly for the sake of Christ and his Word strengthens other Christians in their assurance of the validity of their faith and encourages them in their own witness.

- You should speak or write with graciousness and humility, recalling Paul's word in Colossians 4:6, which may be paraphrased thus: "Let your conversation always be graciously winsome and seasoned with the salt of wit and pungency, so that you may know how you should give an answer, suitable for each occasion and each need, to each individual."

- Remember that our aim is not to win arguments but to win people. It is perilously easy to win the argument but "lose" the person. On the other hand, you may sometimes lose the argument but win over the person, because of your gracious, humble demeanour.

- In public dialogue or debate, whether face-to-face or on radio or TV, your focus should be on the wider audience not your immediate "opponent," and you should prepare memorable "one-liners."

- Decide what is appropriate to say and not to say in the particular situation. Avoid the temptation of saying too much too soon. A full declaration of the gospel or of "the whole purpose of God" (Acts 20:27) is not called for on each occasion! It is significant that when Paul was formally charged by Tertullus in his trial before the governor Felix at Caesarea, he answered the charges against him point by point (Acts 24:1–21). Only afterwards, when invited by Felix, did Paul speak about "faith in Christ . . . righteousness, self-control and the judgment to come" (Acts 24:24–25).
- All apologetic efforts should be bathed in corporate prayer.

EVANGELISTIC WRITING

To ensure that the gospel receives as favorable a hearing as possible, I have often used a positive "technique." After I have befriended a check-out person or a supervisor at a supermarket who gives especially good service, or a technician who has carried out house repairs or improvements in a capable way, I write to the employer praising their employee for efficient service given. Then I send a copy of the letter to the employee for their encouragement along with a copy of my book *Three Crucial Questions about Jesus* or *John 3:16* and Nicky Gumbel's *Why Jesus?* indicating that my wife and I are convinced and committed Christians who believe that the most important thing in life is one's relationship with Jesus Christ and providing our telephone number should they wish to chat about these matters. One such person told me excitedly that her employer had put the letter up on the employees' noticeboard. Employers regularly receive complaints but rarely unsolicited words of congratulation, and employees are more likely to respond positively to the Good News if they feel grateful to its bearer.

In 1980 there was widespread controversy in New Zealand because under governmental pressure the film censor disallowed the screening of the film "Death of a Princess" because it would offend Islamic sensibilities at a time when New Zealand was negotiating trade deals with Saudi Arabia. On the other hand, "The Life of Brian," a Monty Python sophisticated parody of the life of Jesus that was a full-scale assault on Christian sensibilities, was passed for screening to those sixteen and over.

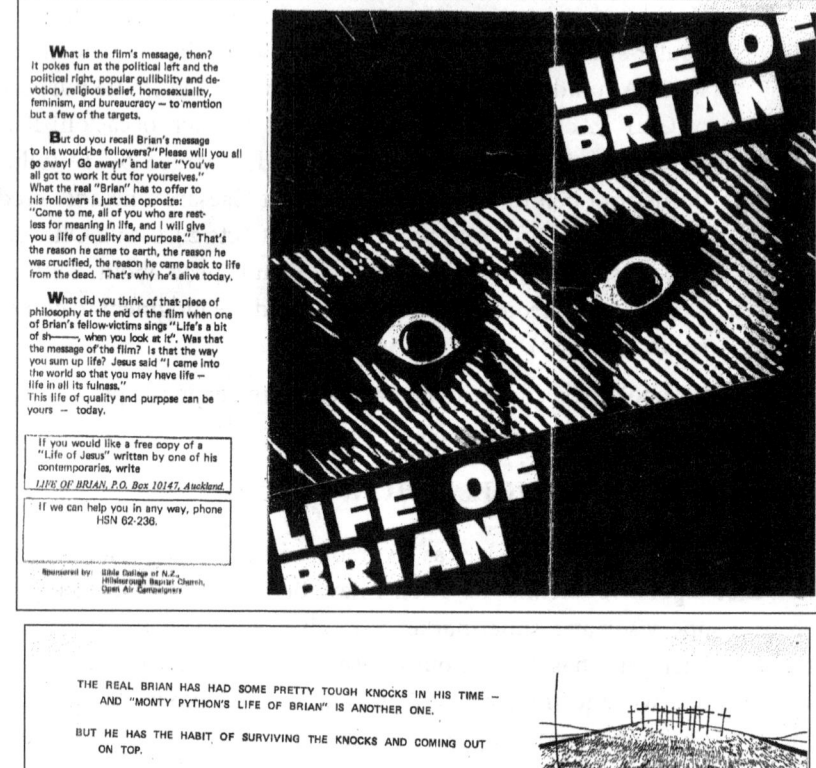

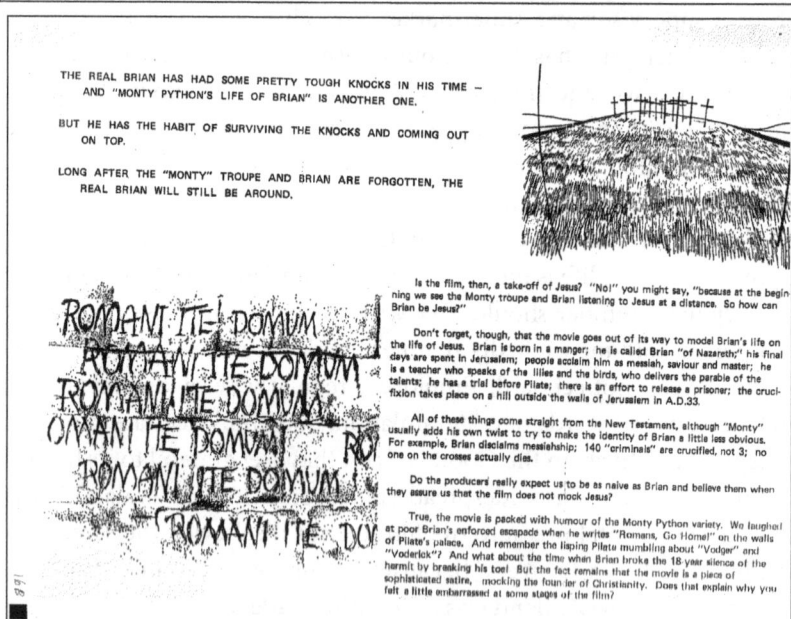

Prior to its release, vigorous opposition had been voiced by various Christian and community groups (such as the Society for the Promotion of Community Standards, Inc.), but to no avail. I realised that many Christians planned to demonstrate outside the theatres where the film was being shown, so I flew down to Wellington to view the film twice (taking notes in the dark!) and with the help of an artist I prepared a tract that interacted with the content of the film, offered a free copy of the Gospel of Luke, and gave a telephone number for any enquiries. City bylaws regarding the distribution of pamphlets in public places were checked, rosters were made out for manning telephones, and I wrote a review of the film for the *Challenge Weekly*. With the cooperation of many local churches in various cities, this tract was distributed to thousands of theatre patrons after they had seen the film. Wellington, for example, ordered ten thousand copies of the brochure and ten churches cooperated in the venture, while Auckland distributed a thousand copies a day at the four daily showings. Instead of negative demonstrations that would merely have increased gate takings, there were multitudes of positive discussions outside theatres, particularly among young people, about the true "Brian of Nazareth." Apologetics and evangelism were blended.

To enable Jennifer to secure a motorised wheelchair, we were visited by an occupational therapist, Geoff Edwards, for several weeks. On his last visit I gave him a copy of *Three Crucial Questions about Jesus*, having discovered he was a keen reader and had experimented with Buddhism. Two weeks later he unexpectedly appeared in church. "I am here because of your book!" Later he explained, "My work takes me into many homes, but the vibes in your home were different." Genuine faith had been born and regular mentoring followed before he married a Christian nurse (I was their "best man" at age seventy!). They now have three delightful children. It was an unexpected delight recently to see Geoff's "Letter to the Editor" in a local paper entitled "Christ the only way to get reconciled to God," written in response to secular correspondence on the matter. What pleasure can compete with seeing God at work?

11

Happy Memories

FAMILY

I HAVE SKETCHED THE extraordinary circumstances that led to our adoption of Oliver in 1973 and of Jane in 1979 (see above, chapters 4 and 6). Our excitement and pride were increased when Oliver married Bianca in 2004 and Liam was born a year later, and Jane married Aaron in 2001 with Alexandria born in 2007 and Greyson in 2013. We eagerly look forward to the visits of Oliver or Bianca with Liam from Takaka in the South Island, and the regular visits of Jane and Aaron and their family from Parakai north of Auckland.

COLLEAGUES

A teacher becomes enriched not only by the questioning or even cross-questioning of students but also by the stimulating friendship and gentle criticism of colleagues. Richard Longenecker was an industrious scholar who provided a model for me to emulate and we became fellow toilers on the Committee for Bible Translation that produced the NIV. I was chairman of the NT Department at Trinity when the whirlwind from Canada, Don Carson, touched down in Illinois. He has become well known as the cofounder of the influential Gospel Coalition as well as the author or editor of multitudes of books. As John Woodbridge and I drove home after a faculty meeting he would rollick in laughter at my "take" on proceedings and later we would relax on the tennis court along with David Wells. John is an authority on eighteenth century France and the history of Evangelicalism. It was always stimulating to mix with specialists in Old Testament such as Gleason Archer and Willem van Gemeren, in New Testament such as Walter Liefeld and Grant Osborne, in systematic theology such as Clark Pinnock and Wayne Grudem, and in missiology such as Herb Kane and David Hesselgrave.

As for faculty visitors to Trinity, I recall Leon Morris's skill at table hockey in our home. Nor would one ever forget the delightful grandfatherly gesture of Carl Henry at our home in motioning a young Korean girl to come and sit on his knee to receive his encouragement. How charming to receive a bear hug from John Stott after he had spoken at chapel! "Now," he said consolingly, "you and I have something more in common—being under attack in the US!" And what a compliment to receive a request from Stott for a copy of my chapel address on the concept of the impassibility of God.

STUDENTS

It gives any teacher great pleasure to remember past students who have excelled in their chosen field—persons such as the Christian apologist Ravi Zacharias, or Jim Wallis, the founder and editor of *The Sojourners*, or the philosopher and theologian William Lane Craig. Not surprisingly, most of my students went on to pastoral positions in the US, but few can match Ron Lutjens who has served admirably in one church (Old Orchard in Webster Groves, Missouri) for thirty-seven years. Some of my students advanced to doctoral studies elsewhere and then to significant academic posts, such as Bruce Demarest (Denver), Ronald Piper (St Andrews), Scot McKnight (Northern Seminary), and Ross Wagner (Princeton and Duke). But since my specialty is NT Greek, it is a special delight to recall two students who attended several of my Greek classes and have made distinctive contributions in this field. Douglas J. Moo has penned commentaries showing mastery of the Greek text (Romans, James, Colossians and Philemon, Galatians, 2 Peter and Jude) and now serves as chair of the NIV Committee on Bible Translation. Michael W. Holmes took Beginning Greek with me in the summer of 1974, and has now produced the standard work *The Apostolic Fathers. Greek Texts and English Translations* (2007, third edition). Then outside my NT field, three students took my class on the Greek Old Testament (LXX) and now hold professorial posts in Old Testament—Richard Shultz, Duane A. Garrett and Richard S. Hess.

For good reason, I enjoyed special rapport with international students. One such student, David M. Kasali, completed his doctoral dissertation under my supervision and then for eight years served as the Principal and later Vice Chancellor of Nairobi Evangelical Graduate School of Theology. In 2014 he was honored by the Scholar Leader of the Year award at the Great Lakes Initiative gathering in Uganda in recognition of his role as Founder and President of the Université Chrétienne Bilingue du Congo (Christian Bilingual University of Congo). At one stage at Trinity there were one hundred and twenty students and their wives from Korea, all of them highly motivated and diligent in their studies. Two of them already had doctorates in aeronautical engineering. Dr Steven C. H. Chang, once my graduate and teaching assistant, has been Professor of New Testament since 2011 at Torch Trinity Graduate University in Seoul, Korea, and now is also Dean of Academic Planning there. One pair of Korean men agreed that on one day each week they would speak only Greek until lunchtime, as a way of improving their facility in the language. In my Beginning Greek class we always recited the Lord's Prayer in Greek until a Japanese student, Hiroo Kambe, who had majored in music converted the Prayer into music so that we could sing it that way. Subsequently a New Zealander did the same for Philippians 2:5–11, another passage we used to memorise in Beginning Greek.

NEW INTERNATIONAL VERSION (NIV) INVOLVEMENT

There were four major steps in the production of the NIV.

1. The translation team that produced the initial draft of each Biblical book;
2. the Intermediate Editorial Committee;
3. the General Editorial Committee, where the expertise of stylists in English were brought in;
4. the Committee on Bible Translation (CBT), the group of twelve to fifteen scholars, representing a range of denominations and nationalities and expertise in Old and New Testament studies and Christian theology, who were responsible for the final translation.

A colleague from Trinity Dr Paul E. Leonard and I produced the first draft of Colossians (1971), while another Trinity friend Dr Richard N. Longenecker and I worked on Ephesians (also 1971). At the Intermediate level, I worked with others in reviewing parts of Romans and Hebrews. From 1984 to 1996 I served on the CBT, and at the same time was secretary of the British subcommittee that converted American English into the purity of the Queen's English! Also I was the CBT representative in the initial discussions about a Spanish NIV.

At the team translation stage we worked at the rate of about three verses an hour, but of course the speed increased in the review stages. At the CBT stage we paused as long as needed over single words or phrases. I vividly remember our spending half an hour on one occasion discussing whether or not to include a comma! Although I was the only person from Australia or New Zealand on the CBT, no one (thus far) has discovered a Kiwi flavor in any of the NIV renderings. In 1979 the *NZ Herald* ran quite an extensive article under the heading, "Aucklander helped to translate new Bible."

Clearly, then, the NIV is the product of committee work. But what is so beneficial about translations done by committees?

- No single scholar could possibly be up to date with the latest developments in the understanding of the grammar and textual criticism of Biblical Hebrew, Aramaic and Greek. When the expertise of scholars in various fields is pooled, the translation that results must be more satisfactory than one that depends on the scholarship of a single person. In fact, committee work is beneficial in promoting humility. Your peers—not your students—evaluate your work. For example, only seven of my sixteen proposals for the revision of 2 Corinthians were adopted by the committee. Only fourteen of my forty-one suggestions for changes in the 1978 edition of the whole NT were accepted. And after I had completed a requested study of the NIV renderings of the various tenses of the verb *pisteuō* ("believe"), only seven of twenty-five proposals were adopted after discussion.

- Personal preferences or biases of an ecclesiastical or theological nature are avoided in a committee enterprise.

- In the give and take of vigorous committee discussion, translation problems are more readily solved than in private study and reflection.

But there are disadvantages to the committee approach. The flashes of insight or brilliance and the happy phrases that mark an individual's translation—I am thinking of the work of James Moffatt, E. J. Goodspeed, R. A. Knox, J. B. Phillips and Henry Cassirer—are generally extinguished in a committee situation. Or again, a committee generally imposes a stylistic uniformity on a translation. In the case of the NT, there were some nine different authors with widely differing Greek styles, ranging from the straightforward, unsophisticated style of Mark to the rugged forcefulness of Paul or the pleasing elegance of 1 Peter. But most English versions of the NT have a uniform committee style.

We took our work with great seriousness—after all, we were destined to be influencing the history of the English Bible—yet there were moments of irrepressible hilarity as someone realised what he had just proposed in the cut and thrust of dialogue. Take the case of the verb "practise (practice in the US)." A doctor practises his profession of medicine, while a footballer practises his moves. In the former case, "practise" means "carry out; "in the latter, "try to improve." What, then, if someone proposes to render *mēde porneuōmen* in 1 Corinthians 10:8 by "let us not practise/practice immorality"! We were not laughing at the sacred text but at our puny efforts to render it in our ambiguous language. In this case an appropriate rendering is "Let us not indulge in immorality" (NAB) or "Nor let us not act immorally" (NASB) or "We should not commit sexual immorality" (NIV).

Speaking of the English Bible, in the mid-1980s after three hundred and fifty years of King James Version (KJV)/Authorised Version (AV) dominance, the NIV eclipsed the KJV as the most popular English translation of the Bible. How could English speakers of the twentieth—or twenty-first-century understand the KJV version of Psalm 119:147, "I prevented the dawning of the morning," or 2 Thessalonians 2:7, "He who now letteth will let," unless they have a specialized knowledge of seventeenth-century English? Two of the distinctives in preparing the NIV for publication were the widespread testing of preliminary drafts on young and old, educated and uneducated, and the evaluation of the version for reading silently or reading in church.

Happy Memories

Committee on Bible Translation

John Stek, Bruce Waltke, Larry Walker, Walter Liefeld, Ken Barker,
Ron Youngblood, Laird Harris—Donald Madvig, Dick France,
Donald Wiseman, Murray Harris, Dick Longenecker

British subcommittee of Committee on Bible Translation

Howard Marshall, Earle Kalland, Donald Wiseman,
Murray Harris, Martin Selman

CREATION OF TYNDALE COLLEGE (TC) IN NEW ZEALAND

"University graduates are often God's frozen assets." It was my belief in this aphorism that led to the creation of Tyndale College in 1980. They are "assets" because they have distinctive God-given gifts that have been highly developed. These assets are often "frozen" because the giftedness of these graduates has not been recognised or used in the local church. Part of this failure is that these graduates themselves have not closed the gap between their professional competence and their knowledge of the Faith that would enable them to contribute distinctively to the life of the church. TC, then, was designed to help thaw out these assets. What was needed was not simply advanced Bible study but the scholarly study of the Scriptures and Christian theology and history at a university level. So students enrolled as part-time extra-mural candidates for the postgraduate Bachelor of Divinity degree (BD) from the examining body the Melbourne College of Divinity (MCD) that was affiliated with the University of Melbourne and had been constituted by parliamentary Act of the State of Victoria, Australia, in 1910.

In orientation TC was unashamedly academic, a community of those committed to the pursuit of academic excellence in the field of Biblical studies and theology for the sake of God's Kingdom and the local church. Its motto was taken from the apostle Paul's injunction in 1 Corinthians 14:20: "*Tais phresin teleioi ginesthe*" ("Be mature in your understanding"). In keeping with the character of the College as a post-graduate study centre, all the weekly classes (except beginning language courses) were conducted as seminars in which students read and discussed one another's research papers under the guidance of the tutor. Any tutorial lectures that introduced a subject were non-sectarian in nature and sought to heighten awareness of our rich Christian heritage. In theological stance the College reflected an informed conservative Protestantism, with a doctrinal basis the same as that of the Tertiary Students' Christian Fellowship. The Board of the College was composed of four student representatives, two representatives of the TSCF, two from the BCNZ (one from their Board, one from their faculty), one representative of the wider Christian public, and the Registrar.

[Handwritten-edited typescript of Romans 3:24–31, dated Oct. 1970, Team Trans.]

The College, named in honor of William Tyndale (c.1494–1536), the celebrated reformer and translator, was not created without some controversy. It was said that I could not serve two masters—BCNZ and TC. But I regarded TC as a voluntary part-time venture of my own, not compromising or competing with my full-time responsibility at BCNZ. When I left BCNZ in 1981, the duties of registrar and tutor of TC were ably assumed by (now Dr) Philip Church who guided the College until 2000 when MCD discontinued examining for the BD degree. At that stage the BCNZ assumed the name "Tyndale" for its graduate section, thus the Tyndale Graduate School of Theology. From 2006 until 2011, in partnership with Carey Baptist College, it became Tyndale—Carey Graduate School, and then with the name change of BCNZ it was renamed Laidlaw—Carey Graduate School. Finally, in 2011 after Carey gained approval for its own master's programme, it became Laidlaw Graduate School that itself was incorporated within Laidlaw's School of Theology in 2015.

During the twenty years of the College's operation (1980–2000), some twenty-three men and women successfully completed their BD studies.

That number may seem insignificant until one remembers the strategically important positions that some of the graduates held or hold. For example, Dr Warren Brookbanks, Professor of Law at the University of Auckland and then the Auckland University of Technology; Dr David Richmond, retired Professor of Medicine and Medical Education at the University of Auckland; Jenni Broom, QSO, formerly National Coordinator of the NZ Refugee and Migrant Service; Dr Ian Payne, formerly Principal, Pathways College of Bible and Mission, and South Asia Institute of Advanced Christian Studies (SAIACS); Dr Ian Stewart, Director of Faculty Development, Stern School of Business, New York University; Dr John de Waal, plastic surgeon; Murray Burt, Global Infrastructure Manager for the United Nations High Commissioner for Refugees (UNHCR).

The testimony of Professor Richmond is typical. "Tyndale studies consumed much of my leisure time for five years (1989–1994). Two things motivated me to continue: an appreciation of the quality of the course, and a growing awareness of the importance of what I was doing. The college provides an intellectually stimulating yet spiritually satisfying approach to Biblical and theological studies."

LIBRARY GIFT TO THE NAIROBI EVANGELICAL GRADUATE SCHOOL OF THEOLOGY (NEGST)

It is very tempting for teachers of graduate students to make special provision for their retirement by selling their personal library, built up over many years, to a local institution that already has considerable library holdings. But having been closely associated with international students in my teaching at Trinity—and being an international myself—I believed it would be strategically important to gift my library to some "two-thirds world" theological seminary. Since one of my doctoral students (Dr David Kasali) was returning to Kenya as Principal of NEGST, it was natural that I should offer the library to his school. So it was that in 1996 just before our return to NZ we contacted the Overseas Council in the US who generously agreed to pack up and despatch the five thousand six hundred books and seven hundred journals. The Director of Research at the Overseas Council commented that the gift "will make NEGST the best equipped New Testament research library on the African continent." Then in 2015 the Leadership Development—Langham Partnership in NZ fulfilled this same service for a further one thousand four hundred volumes. An insert was pasted inside each of the seven thousand volumes indicating that the books were given in honor of Rev Zefania Kasali (1915–1996), David's father, who had been a pioneering evangelist and pastor in Kenya.

It gave us great pleasure to know that the books were being given a second life in an institution (now part of Africa International University) committed to the preparation of leaders for the African Church. To cap off the donation, Jennifer provided two magnificent nine-foot high quilted banners reading "Look up at the heavens and count the stars" and "Yours, O Lord, is the greatness and the power."

Murray and Jennifer with
Dr. David Kasali

PUBLISHER'S PREFACE IN THE EXEGETICAL GUIDE TO THE GREEK NEW TESTAMENT (EGGNT)

Mention has already been made of the motivation behind this series of NT commentaries (chapter 10, p. 66). The initial volume on *Colossians & Philemon* in the projected twenty volumes covering the whole NT was published by Eerdmans in 1991. It was greatly encouraging to have warm recommendations on the cover from Professors Moule, Metzger, Dunn, and Dr Stephen Olford and then positive reviews from a wide theological spectrum of reviewers. I had hoped to produce another volume promptly but found I was preoccupied with other writing projects, especially my commentary on the Greek text of 2 Corinthians whose preparation spanned twenty-five years. For their part, editors at Eerdmans were beginning to doubt whether there would continue to be a market for such specialist commentaries. Simultaneously I learned that Broadman & Holman, the publishing wing of the Southern Baptist Convention, were planning to enter the academic market more vigorously, so protracted negotiations began with this new publisher and a revised edition of *Colossians and Philemon* appeared in 2010. A variety of international authors have been contracted to complete the series. At the time of writing nine of the projected twenty volumes have appeared.

It came as a total—but pleasant—surprise to be informed by B & H Academic that each new volume will include a "Publisher's Preface" that reads as follows.

> It is with great excitement that we publish this volume of the Exegetical Guide to the Greek New Testament series. When the founding editor, Dr Murray J. Harris, came to us seeking a new publishing partner, we gratefully accepted the offer. With the help of the coeditor, Andreas J. Köstenberger, we spent several years working together to acquire all the authors we needed to complete the series. By God's grace we succeeded and contracted the last author in 2011. Originally working with another publishing house, Murray's efforts spanned more than twenty years. As God would have it, shortly after the final author was contracted, Murray decided God wanted him to withdraw as coeditor of the series. God made it clear to him that he must devote his full attention to taking care of his wife, who faces the daily challenges caused by multiple sclerosis.
>
> Over the course of many years, God has used Murray to teach his students how to properly exegete the Scriptures. He is an exceptional scholar and professor. But even more importantly, Murray is a man dedicated to serving Christ. His greatest joy is to respond in faithful obedience when his master calls. "There can be no higher and more ennobling privilege than to have the Lord of the universe as one's Owner and Master and to be his accredited representative on earth" (M. J. Harris, *Slave of Christ: A New Testament Metaphor for Total Devotion to Christ* [Downers Grove:

InterVarsity, 1999, 155]). Murray has once again heeded the call of his master.

It is our privilege to dedicate the Exegetical Guide to the New Testament series to Dr Murray J. Harris. We pray that our readers will continue the work he started.

(Reproduced with permission) B&H Academic

SUPPORT OF NEEDY CHILDREN

We have been privileged, for over fifty years, to support individual children in the so-called "Two-Thirds World" through the efficient services of World Vision and the TEAR fund. It has always been a special pleasure to receive the children's letters (translated by a local helper) and pictures, sometimes along with photos of them, and then to send them news of our family and assurance of our prayer for them. Our most recent "child," now a young woman, is able to support herself after ten years of being supported and is pursuing professional studies in accountancy. And through the Barnabas Fund we continue to support a needy Christian family in Pakistan.

The Library of the Nairobi Evangelical Graduate School of Theology that received Murray's 7000 volumes and 700 journals

BILLY GRAHAM CAMPAIGN

With the passing of Dr Billy Graham, memorabilia relating to his campaigns become more precious. I treasure my small official counsellor's badge for the Auckland campaign at Carlaw Park in 1959 that I wore proudly as a twenty-year old. All potential counsellors had undergone special training, in my case at Ngaire Avenue Chapel in Newmarket. Strangely, I had recently attended an athletics event at this Park to watch what turned out to be a record-breaking run over four hundred yards by a renowned international sprinter. But now vastly different records were being broken—the numbers attending the meetings, and the numbers of those professing faith in Christ. During Graham's campaign meetings at the Park, nearby steam trains that went up quite a steep incline were cancelled lest they drown out the sound system! It was enthralling to be not only a witness but part of God's saving action through his servant.

MOVE TO A RETIREMENT VILLAGE

In 2017 we felt the time was appropriate to move into a "lifestyle" retirement village. Care for a property as well as for a home and an invalid wife was proving too taxing for me. After investigating all the possibilities in surrounding areas, we opted for Alandale Retirement Village that is delightfully situated on the Waikato River in Hamilton, where there are two-bedroom villas each having "unit title," meaning that one's villa is owned by the resident, not by some corporation answerable to shareholders. One attractive feature of the village is a large heated swimming pool where I can maintain my fitness.

12

Painful Memories

DEATH OF OUR DAUGHTER SUSAN

I HAVE ALREADY SKETCHED the circumstances of Susan's death in connection with our desire to apply for an adoption (chapter 4, pp. 29-30). Born prematurely at twenty-six weeks, Susan lived for only six hours fifty minutes. I saw her in an incubator only at a distance and only for a few fleeting minutes. Jennifer never saw her, for she was unconscious at that time as she began her recovery from fulminating toxaemia.

I remember being overcome with grief as I wheeled the small coffin into the lounge of Jennifer's parents' home where we were staying and where the family funeral was held. Our pastor at Tamaki Bible chapel, Balfour Jacobsen, conducted the service, reminding us that in all his actions God is too inherently wise to be mistaken and too intrinsically good to be unkind. Susan was buried in the infants' plot at Mangere Lawn Cemetery where her paternal grandparents are also buried. We look forward to seeing and recognising Susan in her prime in a resurrection body. If, during his earthly life Jesus restored wholeness when he healed people, how much more in the eternity of the life to come will he bring to the wholeness of maturity children who have died in infancy including those who are born prematurely and then die.

Painful Memories

JENNIFER'S DIAGNOSIS OF MULTIPLE SCLEROSIS (MS)

It was by an MRI scan in 1991 that Jennifer was confirmed as having multiple sclerosis. Numbers of strange symptoms such as numbness, blurred vision, dizziness and decreasing mobility that Jennifer had been experiencing were explained by this diagnosis, so that in one sense the diagnosis brought a certain relief.

MS is an inflammatory disease of the central nervous system. The casing around the nerves leading to the brain has become damaged or hardened (hence *sclerosis*, the Greek term for "hardening") in many places (hence "multiple"). Given the difficulty that messages have in travelling to the brain, MS can adversely affect every part and function of the body. Strangely, the prevalence of MS increases the further away one gets from the equator, a fact that supports the hypothesis that sunlight levels may be a crucial factor in the risk of developing MS. In NZ the prevalence of MS is seventy-two per one hundred thousand people, seventy-five percent being women and twenty-five percent men, giving a female to male ratio of 3:1. Of the three major types of MS, about fifty percent have the relapsing—remitting type, about twenty percent primary progressive, and about thirty percent secondary progressive, the final stage (the type Jennifer now has). We were told (by a reliable source) that in the USA ninety-five percent of marriages in which one partner has MS end in divorce.

Generally speaking, a person dies with MS, not from MS. So the challenge of living with MS is coping with its unpredictable symptoms that range from a relatively innocuous numbness to the horrific trigeminal neuralgia, the "suicide pain" that affects the nerves of the face and is recognized in medical circles as the most dreadful pain known to humans.

Over the past thirty years Jennifer has shown a remarkable resilience in coping with her MS—not to speak of her inimitable smile—thanks to the concern and prayers of friends around the world (there is twenty-four-hour coverage!) and the ever-present grace of God. As she remembers her years of caring for and entertaining others, now her challenge is patiently to let her husband do the meals, washing and shopping without being able to help. The daily assistance we have for showering and dressing Jennifer, provided by the government sponsored Health Care NZ, is superlative. What a delight it is to hear Jennifer and her friendly helper singing hymns while Jennifer is being showered! And, given Jennifer's artistic skill, she finds great pleasure in making small colorful quilts for babies born prematurely, quilts distributed by the neo-natal unit at a local hospital.

Sample quilts for premature babies

THE DR NORMAN L. GEISLER CONTROVERSY

This unpleasant saga spanned the years 1988 to 1992 although Dr Geisler had raised questions about my view of the resurrection after our return to Trinity in 1986. A history of the controversy is found in chapter XIX of my book *From Grave to Glory. Resurrection in the New Testament. Including a Response to Norman L. Geisler.* In its essence the issue related not to the fact of Christ's resurrection, but to the nature of his resurrection body. To accommodate the wide range of NT data that speak of Christ's becoming invisible as well as being visible after his resurrection, should we speak of his resurrection body as "material," "physical," "fleshly," "supermaterial," "substantial," "supernatural," or "spiritual"? Even at the outset of the controversy, I wrote to President Kenneth Meyer (June 17, 1988):

> "I am happy to reaffirm that I believe that our Lord rose from the dead in the actual, physical body he possessed before his death but that as a result of his resurrection there was an alteration and enhancement of the properties of that physical body so that he now possesses what Paul calls a "spiritual body" (1 Cor 15:44–49) or a "glorious body" (Phil 3:21). Before the resurrection, the body of Jesus was mortal (Mk. 15:37; Col 1:22); through the resurrection, the body of Jesus became immortal (Rom 6:9; Heb 7:16; Rev 1: 18)."

In connection with my reappointment to Trinity, my nomination for tenure, and the investigation of my views, Dr Thomas A. McDill, President of the Evangelical Free Church of America (EFCA) (to which Trinity belongs), observed that some sixty people and nine committees had investigated my views. The consensus was that my "view of the resurrection, although unusual, falls within the parameters of Biblical and historic orthodoxy." Perhaps the most significant committee was one comprising Dr Millard Erickson of Bethel Seminary, Dr Bruce Demarest of Denver Seminary, and Dr Roger Nicole of Gordon-Conwell Seminary. Their unanimous conclusion was that "his (Dr Harris's) views are compatible with the doctrinal position of TEDS, the EFCA and the wider evangelical movement." Such a verdict comports with the view of James I. Packer that "Harris is undoubtedly in the mainstream of resurrection faith" or James Montgomery Boice: "His position is certainly within the bounds of orthodoxy" (both comments are found in their recommendations for *From Grave to Glory*). Packer also commented that "the whole church benefits from the necessity laid on Professor Harris to prove his orthodoxy in the matter of resurrection. This is a clear, warm-hearted book, impeccable in scholarship and inspiring to read."

Why, then, the prolonged debate? I suspect that many were unaware of the complexity and mystery of the NT witness about Christ's resurrection body—the fact that he could appear and disappear at will. Without justification, some claimed there were similarities between my views and those of Jehovah's Witnesses, with the result that my views were declared "cultic" and that by not repudiating me the EFCA was endorsing cultic views! As many as thirty-five "counter-cultic" organizations or individuals joined in this accusation that I was not only unorthodox but "cultic."

For those who had been aware of the Bishop of Durham affair in the UK (see above, chapter 10, pp. 67-68), it was a remarkable anomaly that someone who had so recently and so vigorously argued for the physical resurrection of Jesus should now in the US be accused of denying the bodily resurrection of Jesus. In his trenchant *Christianity Today* review of *From Grave to Glory* and *the Battle for the Resurrection* (N. L. Geisler), John G. Stackhouse, Jr speaks of "the utter preposterousness of Geisler's charges" (concerning Harris's views).

How does one react when falsehoods about one's views are propagated by a fellow believer on a major Christian radio station whose broadcasts are heard on ninety-five satellite stations across the US? The demeanor of Jesus described in 1 Peter 2:23 became my constant model to imitate during those five long years. "When they insulted him (Jesus), he did not retaliate; when he suffered, he made no threats. Instead, he kept entrusting himself to the One who judges justly." In fact, when students in class asked me about the issue, I would lead them in prayer, invoking God's blessing on Dr Geisler, one of God's influential servants.

What was most distressing about this whole episode was the massive amount of time and effort expended by many people over several years. But hopefully an appreciation of the reality and wonder of Christ's resurrection was deepened for many.

It is a pleasure to note that in January 1996 "An Announcement of Resolution" was made, indicating that the then President of the EFCA, Dr Paul Cedar, and its Board of Directors representing Trinity College and TEDS, along with Duane Magnani, President of Witness, Inc. representing the countercult coalition, and Dr Norman Geisler, concurred in declaring that Jesus Christ was raised up in his physical body, that the bodily, physical resurrection of Jesus is essential to the Gospel, and that disagreement between these parties had passed and full reconciliation had taken place.

Happily, the issue was not without some comic relief on occasion. For example, a prominent pastor sent me a long letter that included this confession. "*From Grave to Glory* may be the single most productive read I have had since my conversion, excluding the Word itself, of course . . . I started reading it in detail yesterday morning at 6:30 a.m. I came to my office, never shaved or even turned on the lights. Between a breakfast meeting, a staff meeting, various office duties, and an Elders' meeting (I finally shaved at 7:30 p.m.), I was totally captivated by the immensity and glory of the NT record of our Lord's resurrection . . . At about 11p.m. I finished *From Grave to Glory*. I turned to my wife and said, "I want to be resurrected. And, I want to do it NOW!"

13

Disappointments

INTERNATIONAL FELLOWSHIP OF EVANGELICAL THEOLOGIANS (IFET)

SINCE I WAS A member of both the Institute for Biblical Research in the US and the Tyndale Fellowship in the UK, it naturally occurred to me that an academic umbrella group could benefit both existing groups. So was born my proposal for the creation of an International Fellowship of Evangelical Theologians (IFET), whose aim would be to foster and coordinate on a worldwide scale scholarly evangelical research, writing and publication in the areas of Biblical studies and systematic and applied theology. Other groups that might join the Fellowship included the Fellowship of European Evangelical Theologians (FEET), the Australian Tyndale Fellowship, and the Asian Theological Society.

How might these aims be achieved?

1. An annual conference when council members could establish and review an agenda of immediate and future needs in Biblical and theological research, country by country and worldwide, and award the year's research fellowships. Such planning would avoid unnecessary duplication of evangelical writing.

2. The creation of a publishing arm of IFET to publish a new series of monographs by the research fellows, and to sponsor the translation of these monographs and other key volumes into selected major world languages.

3. An expansion or relocation of Tyndale House and its library by the purchase of property in Cambridge that would include suitable accommodation for the research fellows and their families.

A draft of these proposals was circulated to some key figures. John Stott, for example, was enthusiastic, but those who had the resources or connections to implement the idea felt that the time was not suitable for such a major enterprise.

THE NEW TESTAMENT FROM 28 TRANSLATIONS

In my technical writing on the Greek of the NT I have found it very useful over the years to consult Zondervan's *The New Testament From 26 Translations* (1967 and 1985) to find out which versions have a particular rendering, but also occasionally to discover an alternative way of understanding the Greek text. Such a tool is useful for any reader of the NT who has no knowledge of Greek, although there is always the danger that someone will opt for a translation that appeals to their fancy or supports their preconceived ideas or prejudices. But this tool is especially valuable for students studying the Greek text; for pastors preparing sermons who want to shed fresh light on the NT or want to avoid repeating well known renderings; and for scholars writing general works or commentaries on the NT

My proposal for an updated volume included these changes from the original versions.

1. The base text with which the other translations are compared is the Revised Version of 1881 (the most literal and accurate of English translations), not the King James Version of 1611.
2. All twenty-eight versions are renderings (not paraphrases) of the Greek text, not of Latin or Aramaic translations of the Greek text.
3. Most of the twenty-eight versions were produced by committees, but five by individuals (Barclay, Cassirer, Goodspeed, Moffatt, Weymouth).
4. All of the translations are either commonly used, or, if they are now out of print, enjoyed a wide circulation in their time.
5. "Gender-neutral" translations are represented by the NRSV, the REB, and the NIV.

Disappointments

In my submission of the proposal to Zondervan in March 2009, I included a sample involving Romans 8:1–8 and Hebrews 1:1–4 and indicated my willingness to be general editor and a contributor, observing that a team of about ten scholars could produce such a work in three to four years. Their response was that facilities to compare English versions of the NT were now available on the computer (but not twenty-eight versions and not at a glance, would be my response).

Here is an excerpt (Romans 8:3b) from the sample I submitted.

> *God, sending his own Son in the likeness of sinful flesh*
> . . . who came with a nature like man's sinful nature—GNB
> . . . in a form like that of our own sinful nature—NEB
> . . . with a nature resembling our sinful nature—TCNT
> . . . in a body as physical as any sinful body—JB
> . . . by sending His own Son in flesh like ours under sin's domain—HCSB
> He sent his own Son in a body like the bodies we sinners have—NLT
>
> *and as an offering for sin*
> and to deal with sin—NRSV
> and concerning sin—NET
> and as a sacrifice for sin—NEB
> on account of sin—NKJV
> to atone for sin—TCNT
>
> *condemned sin in the flesh*
> That way God condemned sin in our corrupt nature—GW
> He has passed judgement against sin within that very nature—REB
> He pronounced sentence upon sin in human nature—Wey

INABILITY TO ESTABLISH A REGULAR HOLIDAY VENUE NEAR HOME

When we lived in (NZ's) Cambridge in retirement, I was eager to find a place near home that would regularly give Jennifer a "window on the world" as a temporary alternative to her hospital bed and wheelchair. At Athenree at the north end of the Tauranga Harbour I found a camping ground that would accommodate the campervan we owned at the time. But in spite of our best efforts using a tent attached to the campervan on a reserved site, this desirable alternative accommodation proved to be beyond Jennifer's capacity. So we have become happily accustomed to occasional brief forays throughout the day to local places of interest.

FINDING GOD AT THE UNIVERSITY OF AUCKLAND (?)

When I was speaking at an InterVarsity conference in Michigan, Kelly Monroe (now Kelly Monroe Hullberg) gave me a book she had edited entitled *Finding God at Harvard*. It is a compilation of forty-two testimonials written by Christian faculty and past students at Harvard, indicating their journey of faith and establishing that intellectual credibility and the Christian faith are not incompatible. I wonder whether the title is intentionally ambiguous: How to find God while at Harvard, or Discovering those who follow or followed God while at Harvard?

Would it not be splendid, I thought, if a comparable book were published regarding my Alma Mater ("bounteous mother"), the University of Auckland, particularly since there were numbers of Christian faculty there? My approach to two well-known faculty members was not productive. Perhaps professional pressures prevented additional tasks.

14

Reflections on God and his guidance

In this final chapter I want to share some lessons about God's guidance that I have learned throughout my life. But, first and foremost, I desire to celebrate the magnificent and benevolent character of God as One who rules sovereignly over his children and delights to bring them pleasure.

GOD IS A GOD OF SERENDIPITIES, WHO DELIGHTS TO GIVE US UNEXPECTED, PLEASANT SURPRISES.

My life bears testimony to this truth.

- There have been many and varied opportunities for specialised service— specialised, because for the believer all of life should be regarded as service to the Master: teaching Sunday School classes at Tamaki Bible Chapel; "Bible in Schools" at Glendowie Primary School; Every Boy's Rally at Tamaki Bible Chapel; Children's Special Service Mission (CSSM) at Little Oneroa on Waiheke Island for six years, five as leader; president of the Evangelical Union at Auckland Teachers' College; Crusader Union leader at Glendowie College; Christian Broadcasting Association in Ellerslie; Wycliffe Bible Translators council for three years.
- Financial provision—gifts from friends as we left for study in Manchester; two hundred and fifty pounds from the Wellington Assembly Research Fellowship; seven hundred and fifty pounds

from a Tyndale House research grant; eight thousand (US) dollars for the one year of teaching at Trinity in the midst of studies at Manchester (see chapter 2, p. 21); occasional gifts from Trusts.

- Surprises: adoption of Oliver and Jane (chapters 4 and 6); help with US immigration issues from a friend at Washington Bible College; interview for the *Time* article on miracles; the Murray J. Harris scholarship at Trinity provided by students in my honor; the Publishers' Preface in the EGGNT (chapter 11, pp. 84-85); the offer of free holiday accommodation in Queenstown; the gift of a Toyota Noah van, suitable for Jennifer's wheelchair, given by Christian Trusts on our final return to NZ (chapter 1, p. 6).

GOD IS THE SOVEREIGN LORD, WHO GRACIOUSLY ORCHESTRATES THE DETAILS OF OUR LIVES, SHUTTING SOME DOORS AND OPENING OTHERS.

"I am the LORD your God, who teaches you what is best for you, who directs you in the way you should go" (Isa 48:17).

- When I *applied* for teaching positions, the applications were unsuccessful—a primary school position in the South Pacific in one of NZ's dependencies, to fulfill "country service" requirements and avoid the salary bar; a lecturing position in Religious Studies at Massey University; a post as a lecturer in NT in the University of Manchester (chapter 2, p. 22).

- But again and again I was *offered* suitable positions, but for various reasons I believed I had to decline the offers and continue where I was already happily serving (chapter 4, pp. 32-33). One invitation in particular—to join the Regent College faculty—was very tempting because it might have ultimately led to the creation of a similar institution back in New Zealand.

THE MYSTERY OF GOD'S WILL

None of God's creatures can claim to know all of his will with certainty, but it is much easier to trace his will in retrospect than in prospect. As I reflect now on our difficult decision in 1986 to leave Tyndale House and take up the new challenge at Trinity (see chapter 5), I believe it was the right decision for us and for TH. It was a *difficult* decision because as a family we had enjoyed every aspect of our Cambridge experience and because we had been offered a further term of seven years at TH. With the benefit of hindsight, it was the *right* decision because the move brought us nearer to family in NZ and provided me with more time to devote to research and writing. From the standpoint of TH, our departure was *advantageous* because it enabled a long adjustment in Biblical research to the demands and opportunities of the dawning era of information technology. TH needed Wardens who could pioneer the innovative use of up-to-date IT, not someone who still does not own a cell phone! (I have been forced to use email to enable effective communication with overseas editors. When he heard I was using email, my former student, colleague and friend, Douglas Moo exclaimed, "What is the world coming to? Murray Harris on email!"). Two recent TH projects involving sophisticated IT illustrate the point. STEP stands for Scripture Tools for Every Person, an initiative whose goal is to provide access to a wealth of Biblical resources previously available only to specialist scholars. And in 2017 a new edition of the Greek New Testament was published in the UK by Cambridge University Press and in the USA by Crossway, having been prepared over many years at TH.

In seeking to discover God's will on major matters, there are usually three elements. Throughout the whole process the Spirit will often use Scripture to direct or confirm one's thinking.

1. *Prolonged and disciplined thought and prayer.* We have always drawn up a sheet listing all the pros and cons of the intended decision. Common sense reasoning is crucial. We finally returned to NZ when we did, so as to qualify for superannuation, to be near to family, and because our daughter had just graduated from high school and would be looking for further schooling and employment. And common sense would tell us that, generally speaking, God's call to begin a project is his call to complete it, even if there are delays on the way to the finish. Of necessity, I left my BD study incomplete when we set off for Manchester in 1965. But even after completing my PhD I felt it was beneficial to complete what I had begun, I believed, at God's direction.

2. *The counsel of trusted fellow believers* who know you, your gifts, and your past. I have mentioned my use of well-known advisers in

determining where I should study overseas (p. 16); the recommendation of a friend that led to my first teaching position at Trinity (p. 21); and the letter of encouragement from a friend that prompted my investigation of the opening at TH (p. 49).

3. *The alignment of circumstances,* produced sovereignly by God, that confirms the rightness of the projected decision. We recall the extraordinary circumstances that followed our decision to apply for the adoption of a second child (p. 44). Once approved, we were reminded that usually only one out of three sets of approved parents actually adopt a child, and that there is usually a two to three year waiting period before an adoption—but we received word of Jane's availability less than a week after our letter of approval arrived!

As I have sought to discover and do God's will, my life motto has proved useful in making decisions, large or small.

Omnia sub specie crucis et aeternitatis
"Everything should be seen in the light of the Cross and eternity"

Appendix

CHRONOLOGY

1939	Murray James born to Leslie and Jessie Harris in Birkenhead, Auckland, 19 March, the last of five sons
1952–55	Auckland Grammar School
1956–57	Auckland Teachers' College. President of the Evangelical Union, 1957
1956–60	University of Auckland, part-time, BA in Latin and Greek
1958–65	Teaching at primary schools and a secondary school in Auckland. Involved in Sunday school teaching, Every Boy's Rally, CSSM, and Crusaders
1961	University of Auckland, honours MA in Latin. University of London, extra-mural and part-time, Diploma in Theology, 1960–61
1962	University of Auckland, Diploma in Education
1963	Married to Jennifer Mary McCracken, 28 August
1965–67	University of Manchester, MA → PhD in Biblical Studies
1968–70	
1967–68	Teaching at Trinity Evangelical Divinity School in Deerfield, Illinois, 1971–78 USA, finally as Professor of New Testament Exegesis and Theology
1986–97	
1967–73	NIV translator. Member of the NIV Committee on Bible Translation, 1984–96
1973	Oliver James born in Auckland, 2 November

Appendix

1975	University of Otago, extra-mural and part-time, Bachelor of Divinity
1978–81	Lecturer in New Testament, Bible College of New Zealand
	Member of the NZ Council of Wycliffe Bible Translators
	Founder and Tutor of Tyndale College (now part of Laidlaw School of Theology)
1979	Jessie Jane born in Auckland, 1 March
1981–86	Warden (= Director/Principal) of Tyndale House (a Biblical research library), Cambridge, UK
	Faculty member of The Divinity School, University of Cambridge
1997	Donated most of his technical library (5,600 books and 700 journals) to the Nairobi Evangelical Graduate School of Theology (NEGST) in Kenya (now part of Africa International University)
	Appointed Professor Emeritus, Trinity Evangelical Divinity School/Trinity International University
	Returned to NZ: Auckland (1997–99) → Lake Hawea (1999–2005) → Dunedin (2005–07) → Cambridge (2007–17) – Hamilton (2017 –)
2015	Donated the rest of his technical library (1,400 books) to the Nairobi Evangelical Graduate School of Theology (NEGST) in Kenya

MEMBERSHIP OF LEARNED SOCIETIES

Tyndale Fellowship for Biblical and Theological Research (until 2013)

Elected member of Studiorum Novi Testamenti Societas (SNTS) (since 1984), the premier international body of New Testament scholars

Appendix
SELECTED WRITING

"2 Corinthians" in *The Expositor's Bible Commentary*, Volume 10, ed. F.E. Gabelein (Grand Rapids: Zondervan, 1976) 299–406 (revised 2007)

Appendix on "Prepositions and Theology in the Greek New Testament" in Volume 3 of *The New International Dictionary of New Testament Theology*, ed. C. Brown (Exeter: Paternoster/Grand Rapids: Zondervan, 1978) 1171–1215

Co-editor (with D.A. Hagner) of *Pauline Studies. Essays Presented to Professor F.F. Bruce* (Exeter: Paternoster/Grand Rapids: Eerdmans, 1980)

Raised Immortal. Resurrection and Immortality in the New Testament (London: Marshall, Morgan & Scott, 1983/Grand Rapids: Eerdmans, 1985)

Easter in Durham (Exeter: Paternoster, 1985)

From Grave to Glory: Resurrection in the New Testament (Grand Rapids: Zondervan, 1990; Korean translation, 1995)

Colossians and Philemon (Grand Rapids: Eerdmans, 1991; revised edition, Nashville, TN: Broadman & Holman, 2010)

Jesus as God: The New Testament Use of Theos *in Reference to Jesus* (Grand Rapids: Baker, 1992/Eugene, OR: Wipf & Stock, 2008)

Three Crucial Questions About Jesus (Grand Rapids: Baker, 1994/Eugene, OR: Wipf & Stock, 2008; Greek translation, 1996; Spanish translation, 2005)

The Resurrection of Jesus (Auckland: Affirm Publications, 1998)

Slave of Christ: A New Testament Metaphor for Total Devotion to Christ (Leicester: Apollos, 1999/Downers Grove: InterVarsity, 2001; French translation, 2009)

The Second Epistle to the Corinthians. A Commentary on the Greek Text (Grand Rapids: Eerdmans/Milton Keynes: Paternoster, 2005) in *The New International Greek Testament Commentary* series (ed. I.H. Marshall and D.A. Hagner)

Prepositions and Theology in the Greek New Testament (Grand Rapids: Zondervan, 2012)

Appendix

John 3:16: What's It All About? (Eugene, OR: Wipf & Stock, 2015)

The Gospel of John (EGGNT) (Nashville, TN: Broadman & Holman, 2015)

The Seven Sayings of Jesus on the Cross: Their Circumstances and Meaning (Eugene, OR: Wipf & Stock, 2016)

Studies of Problem Texts and Other Key Verses (2019)

www.ingramcontent.com/pod-product-compliance
Lightning Source LLC
Chambersburg PA
CBHW050841160426
43192CB00011B/2112